Street by Street

PRESTON

C000023533

BAMBER BRIDGE, CHORLEY, LEYLAND, LONGRIDGE

Broughton, Clayton-le-Woods, Coppull, Eccleston, Euxton, Fulwood, Higher Penwortham, Longton, Lostock Hall, Ribbleton, Walton-le-Dale

1st edition August 2003
© Automobile Association Developments Limited 2003

Original edition printed May 2001

Ordnance Survey® This product includes map data licensed from Ordnance Survey ® with the permission of the Controller of Her Majesty's Stationery Office. © Crown copyright 2003. All rights reserved. Licence No: 399221.

Published by AA Publishing (a trading name of Automobile Association Developments Limited, whose registered office is Millstream, Maidenhead Road, Windsor, Berkshire SL4 5GD. Registered number 1878835).

Mapping produced by the Cartography Department of The Automobile Association. (A1709)

A CIP Catalogue record for this book is available from the British Library.

Printed by GRAFIASA S.A., Porto, Portugal

Ref: ML226

Key to map pages	ii-iii
Key to map symbols	iv–1
Enlarged map pages	2-3
Main map pages	4-47
Index – towns & villages	48
Index – streets	49-61
Index – featured places	61-62
Acknowledgements	63

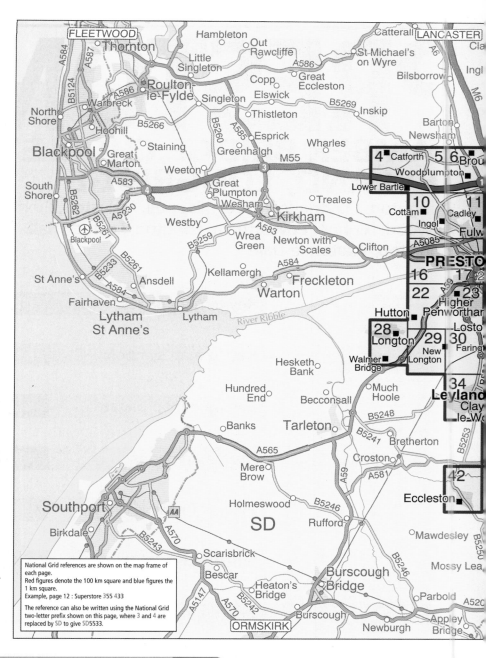

National Grid references are shown on the map frame of each page.
Red figures denote the 100 km square and blue figures the 1 km square.
Example, page 12 : Superstore 355 433

The reference can also be written using the National Grid two-letter prefix shown on this page, where 3 and 4 are replaced by SD to give SD5533.

Scale of enlarged map pages 1:10,000   6.3 inches to 1 mile

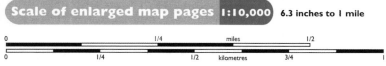

| 0 | 1/4 | miles | 1/2 |
| 0 | 1/4 | 1/2 | kilometres | 3/4 | 1 |

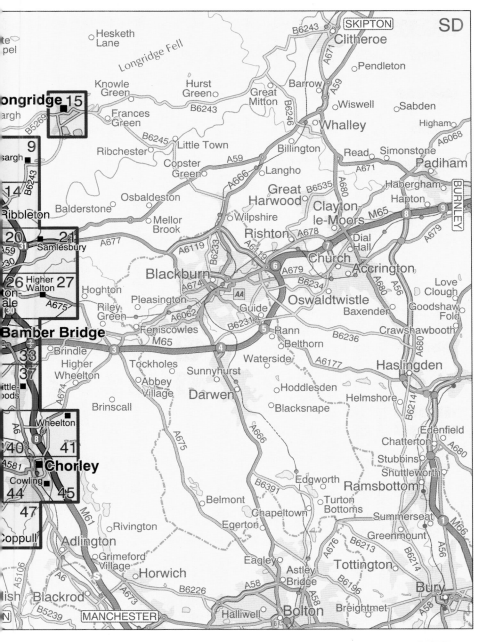

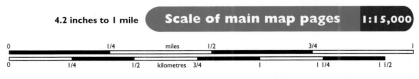

iv

Junction 9	Motorway & junction	Underground station
Services	Motorway service area	Light railway & station
	Primary road single/dual carriageway	Preserved private railway
Services	Primary road service area	Level crossing
	A road single/dual carriageway	Tramway
	B road single/dual carriageway	Ferry route
	Other road single/dual carriageway	Airport runway
	Minor/private road, access may be restricted	County, administrative boundary
	One-way street	Mounds
	Pedestrian area	Page continuation 1:15,000
	Track or footpath	Page continuation to enlarged scale 1:10,000
	Road under construction	River/canal, lake
	Road tunnel	Aqueduct, lock, weir
AA	AA Service Centre	Peak (with height in metres)
P	Parking	Beach
P+	Park & Ride	Woodland
	Bus/coach station	Park
	Railway & main railway station	Cemetery
	Railway & minor railway station	Built-up area

465 Winter Hill

Featured building		Abbey, cathedral or priory	
City wall		Castle	
Hospital with 24-hour A&E department		Historic house or building	
Post Office		Wakehurst Place NT — National Trust property	
Public library		Museum or art gallery	
Tourist Information Centre		Roman antiquity	
Seasonal Tourist Information Centre		Ancient site, battlefield or monument	
Petrol station, 24-hour — Major suppliers only		Industrial interest	
Church/chapel		Garden	
Public toilets		Garden Centre — Garden Centre Association Member	
Toilet with disabled facilities		Garden Centre — Wyevale Garden Centre	
Public house — AA recommended		Farm or animal centre	
Restaurant — AA inspected		Zoological or wildlife collection	
Madeira Hotel — Hotel — AA inspected		Bird collection	
Theatre or performing arts centre		Nature reserve	
Cinema		Aquarium	
Golf course		Visitor or heritage centre	
Camping — AA inspected		Country park	
Caravan site — AA inspected		Cave	
Camping & caravan site — AA inspected		Windmill	
Theme park		Distillery, brewery or vineyard	

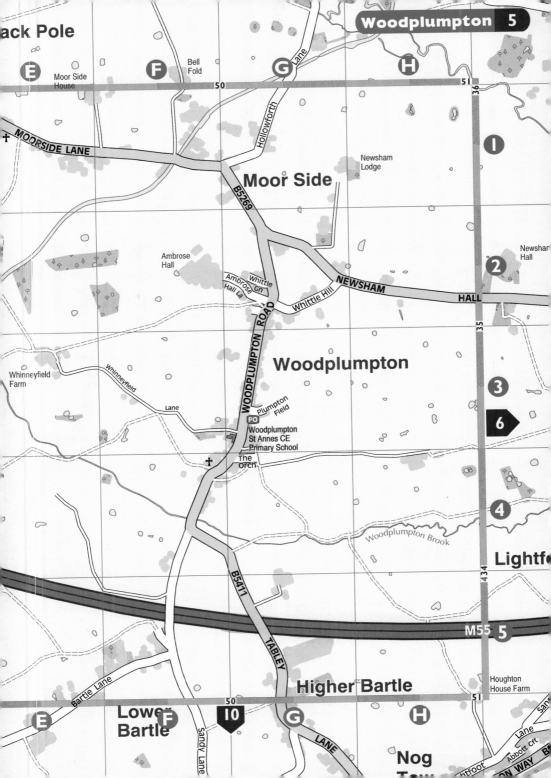

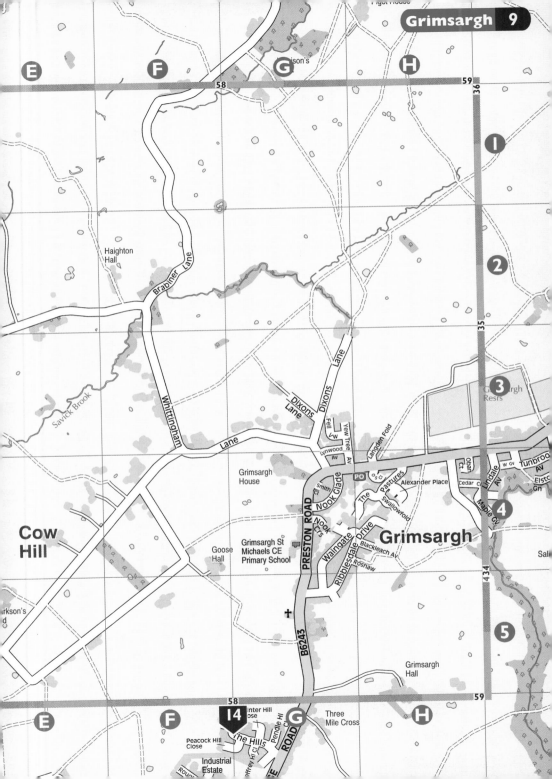

10

A Bartle Lane B **5** 50 C Higher Bartle D

3 49

Lower Bartle

1
tle Hall
tel)

33

Sandy Lane

TABLEY

LANE

Nog Tow

2

Cottam

Hoyles Lane

Honiton Way

Lane

Blennm Way
Sandrm Way

B C

Sidgreaves Lane

32

3 Hoyles Lane

Hoyles

Kingsley Rd

PO

†

Cottam Green
Poppyfield
Meadowbarn Close
Mossb
Cook Dr
Croft
Goldbun Ct
Marifield
B5411

The Gratings

The Chase
Wiltshire Ms
The Grange
The Villas
Miller Lane
Merry Trees Lane
C H L
Whitby Avenue
Estb

The Weald
Spires Gv
Rsd Ct Rosebeł
Av
Cr Wk Rosewood
Mhs Pk
B6241

Hereford Gv
Avon Gardens
Cottam County Primary School
Keats Wy
T Evrgrn
Valentines Meadow
The Gables
Cottam
Millersgate
Dunnock La
Holy Family RC Primary School
Dungon Ci

4 Lea Rd
Lea Endowed CE Primary School
Lea Road

Finch La
Dunnock La
Cottam Way

Ingol Pri School

Westleigh

Dunnock La

Valentines Lane

Cottam Hall Brick Works

5

Lea Road

Preston Sports Arena

Barry

Water's

431

3 49

A Savick Brook B **16** 50 C D

Ashton & Lea Golf Club

Summer Trees Av
Ash Meadow Av
Freshfields
Coppice

Alder Coppice
Wllw Copic
Miller Field
Hazel Coppice
W Mdw
Bilsborough Meadow
Wth Mdw
Savick Way

Savick Way

†
Ain
Arnside Rd
Cartmel
Ashton Primary School
Luton Road West
St Drive
Queensw

1 grid square represents 500 metres

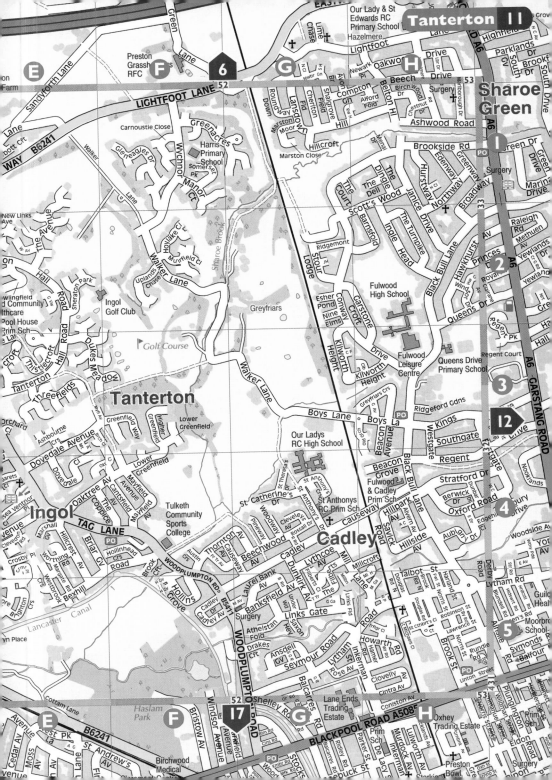

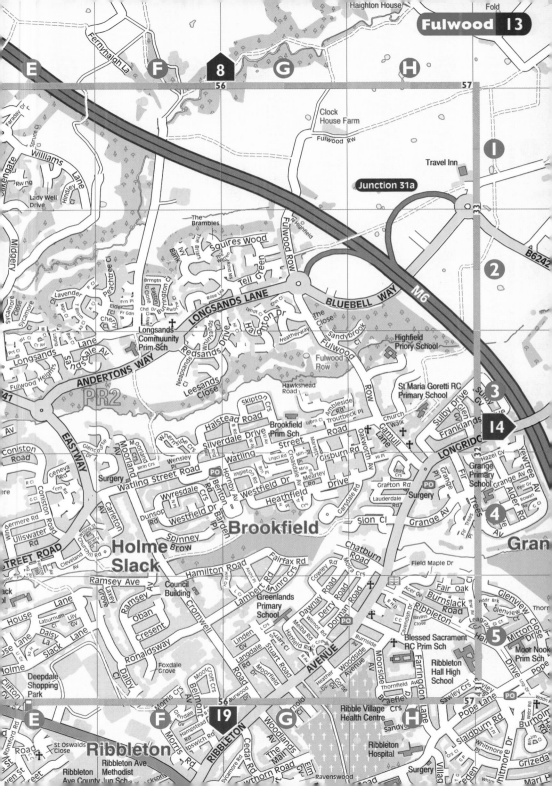

Fold

† B6243

Grimsargh H...

A **B** **9** **C** **D**

3 57 58 59

Winter Hill Close

Three Mile Cross

Pendle Hi Cl

I

...avel Inn

The Hills

Peacock Hill Close

Industrial Estate

Jeffrey Hi Cl

LONGRIDGE ROAD

33

Rough Hey Pl

Rough Hey Road

Roman Way Industrial Estate

Red Scar

Rough Hey Road

Astra Business Centre

2

B6242

B6243

Roman Way

Red Scar Industrial Estate

3

Sulby Drive

...is Drive

Red Scar Industrial Estate

Preston Crematorium

13 LONGRIDGE ROAD

32

Hazel Gv

Yewtree Av

Grange Primary School

Grange Av

Ppir Gv

Rowan

C. Cl

4

...range

Flr

Fir Trees

Alder Rd

Maple Av

Grange

...ple Dr

Fair Oak

Hddr Brk

Glenview Close

Glenview

Thornley Place

Thornley Rd

5

...rnslack Road

...ton

Leagram

Cl Ct

Cl Ct

Mitton Dr

Thornley Rd

Pope La

Pope Lane

River Ribble

...bbleton ...ll High ...chool

Hall

Moor Nook Prim Sch

Pope Lane

Bowland Rd

Birkett Dr

Birkett PI

32

...awley ...rsse Dr

PO

Wddn Rd

Higher Brockholes

Sawley Cr

Pope ...

57

† Brtn Pl

431

Slaidburn Rd

Hazelhurst

Crescent

Whitmore Dr

Crz Cl Cl

A **B** M6 **20** **C** **D**

57 58 59

...edale ...nt

Mari Hill

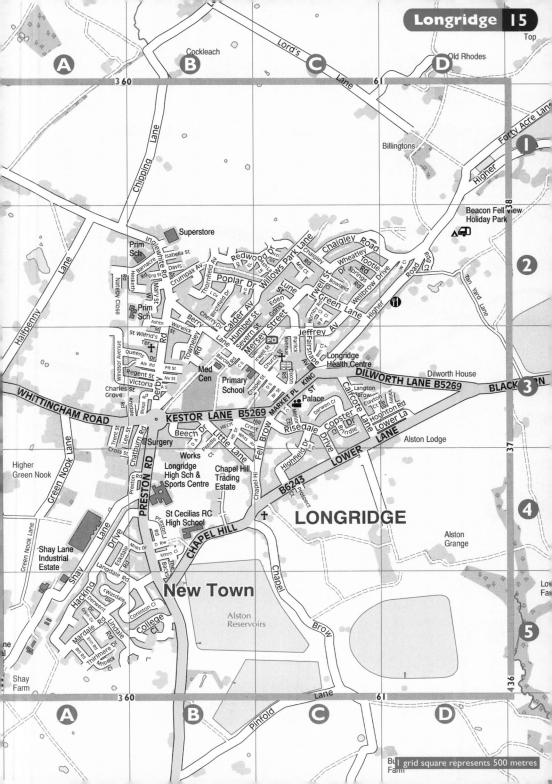

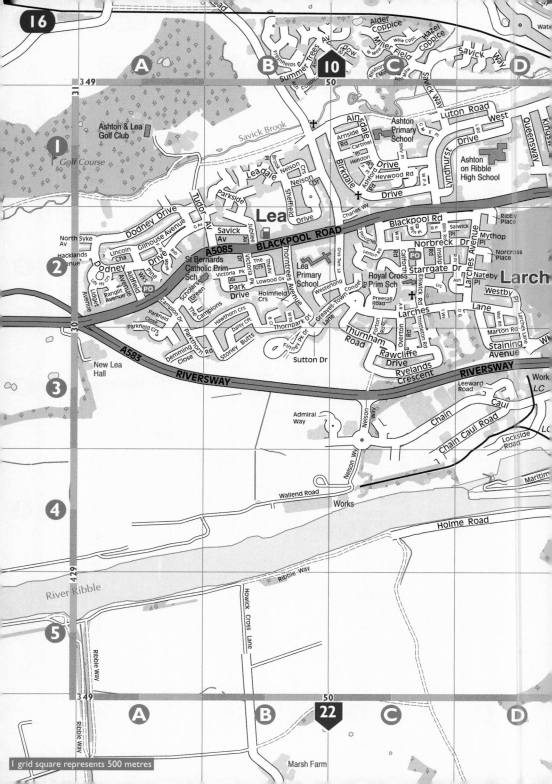

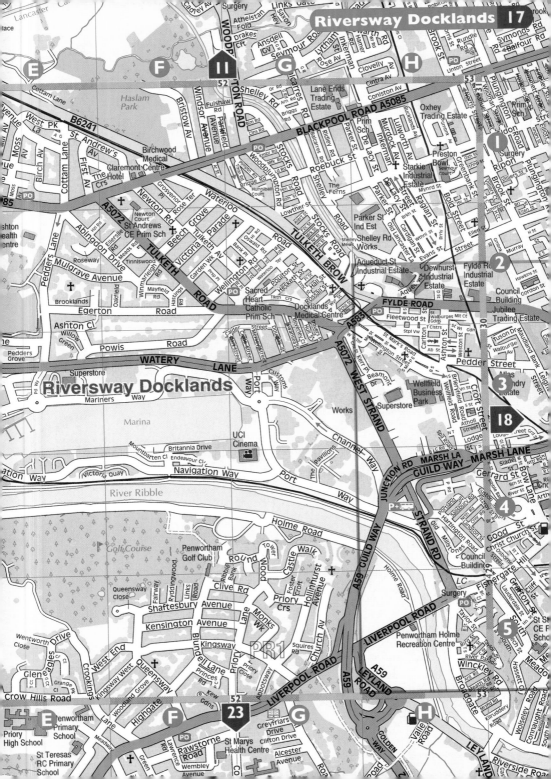

grid square represents 500 metres

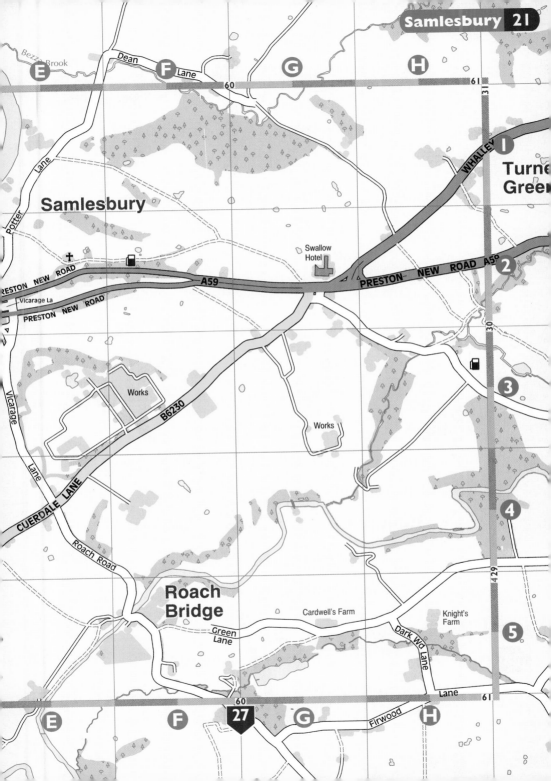

E

Bezza Brook

Dean F Lane

60

G

H

WHALLEY

I

Turner Green

Potter Lane

Samlesbury

✝

Swallow Hotel

PRESTON NEW ROAD A59

2

PRESTON NEW ROAD

A59

30

Vicarage La

PRESTON NEW ROAD

3

Works

Vicarage Lane

B6230

Works

4

CUERDALE LANE

Roach Road

Roach Bridge

Cardwell's Farm

Knight's Farm

Dark Wd Lane

5

429

E

F

60

27

Green Lane

G

Lane

Firwood

H

61

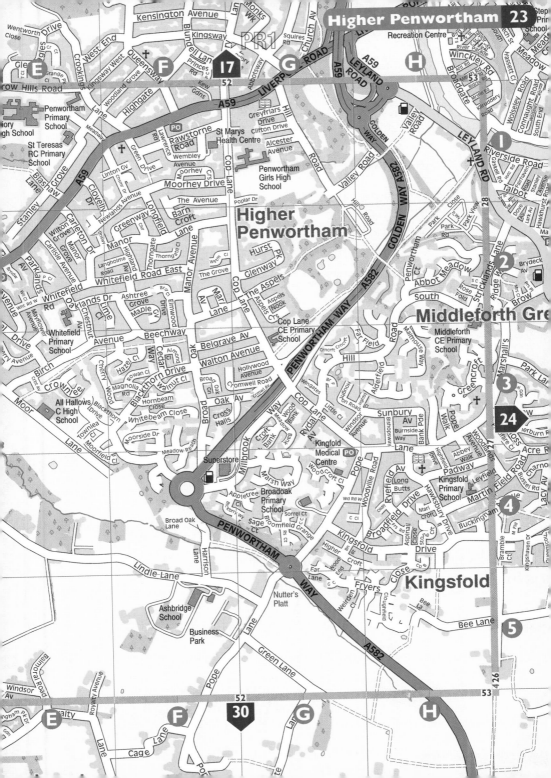

Green Lane

E

F

21

60

G

H

I

Firwood Lane 61

Stanley Grange

28

2

Roach Road

Cripple Gate La

Brook Lane

3

27

Coupe Green Primary School

Green Lane

Methuen Avenue

Manby Close

Mansfield Dr

M Cl

Methuen Dr

Manor Close

Fox Lane

Holker Cl

Carmel Cl Crs

Rusland Dr

Woodhall

Lowick

ys Rd

LANE

Lane

Hall Lane

Quaker

PO

Daub

Bells

Central Avenue

Rhodesway

Lyric Avenue

Squires Close

PO

Larch Gate

Row

Alma Drive

Brch Cl

Gregson

Gregson Lane

Arrowsmith Drive

Knowsley Drive

Knowsley Close

Arrowsmith Close

Mintholme Avenue

Friths Avenue

Brookhouse Close

Brookhouse Drive

Brindle Lodge

Station Rd

LC

The Crossing

Fowler Cl

Fowler Cl

4

Lane

Bourne's field Avenue

LC

Bournesfield

Bourne's Row

Back Bourne's Row

Brindle Gregson Lane Primary School

Brindle St Josephs RC Primary School

E

LC

Bourne's Row

F

60

Cow

G

Hatchwood Farm

426

61

H

Oram Road

Hill House

Lane

Jack Green

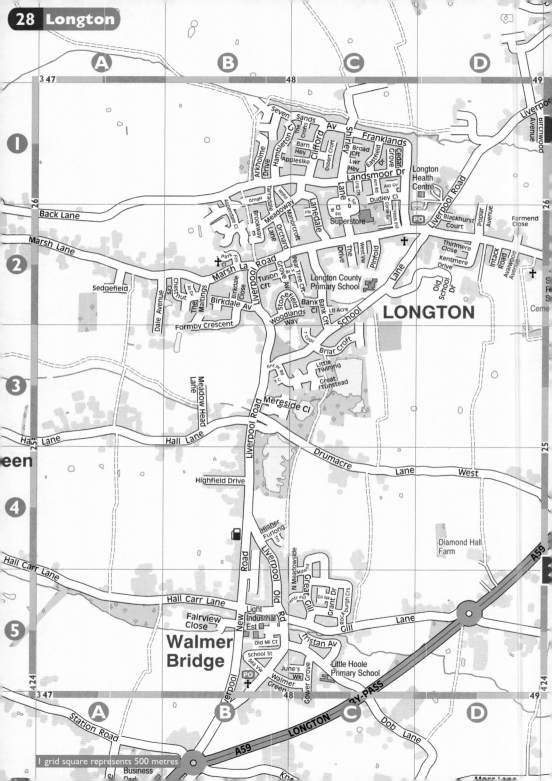

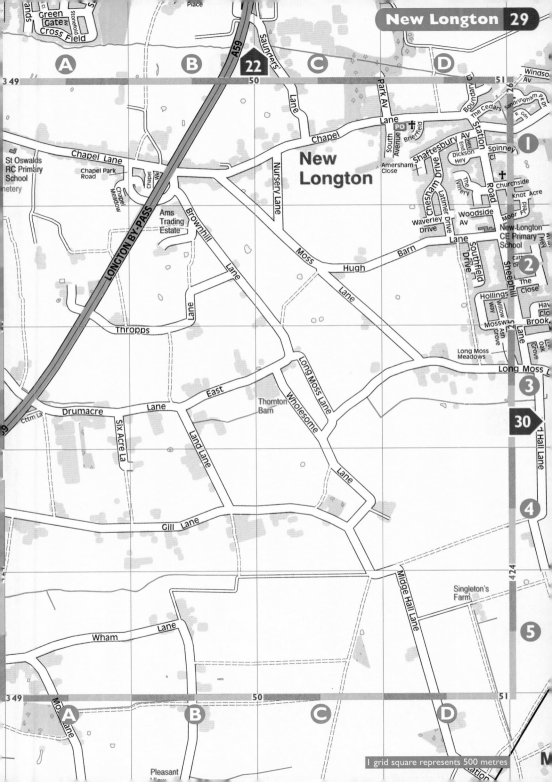

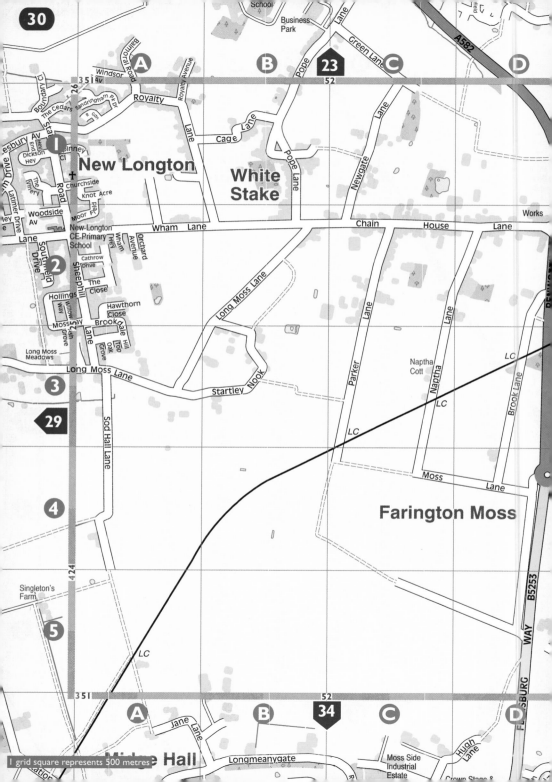

A   **B**   **23**   **C**   **D**

School

Business Park

A582

Windsor

351

Royalty

Pope Lane

Green Lane

52

Royalty Avenue

Balmoral Road

Sandringham Pl Dr

Cage Lane

New Longton

White Stake

Churchside

Knot Acre

Pope Lane

Newgate Lane

Works

Moor

Wham Lane

Chain   House   Lane

Woodside Av

New Longton CE Primary School

Wham Hey

Orchard Avenue

Cathrow Drive

2

Sheephill

The Close

Long Moss Lane

Hollings

Hawthorn Close

Brookdale Hill

Mossway

Willow Way

Top Oak Grove

Lane

Parker Lane

Naptha Cott

Naptha Lane

LC

Brook Lane

Long Moss Meadows

Long Moss Lane

Startley Nook

LC

LC

3

Sod Hall Lane

LC

Moss   Lane

4

Farington Moss

424

Singleton's Farm

B5253

5

LC

351

52

A   **B**   **34**   **C**   **D**

Jane Lane

Longmeanygate

FLENSBURG WAY

Hugh Lane

Midge Hall

Moss Side Industrial Estate

1 grid square represents 500 metres

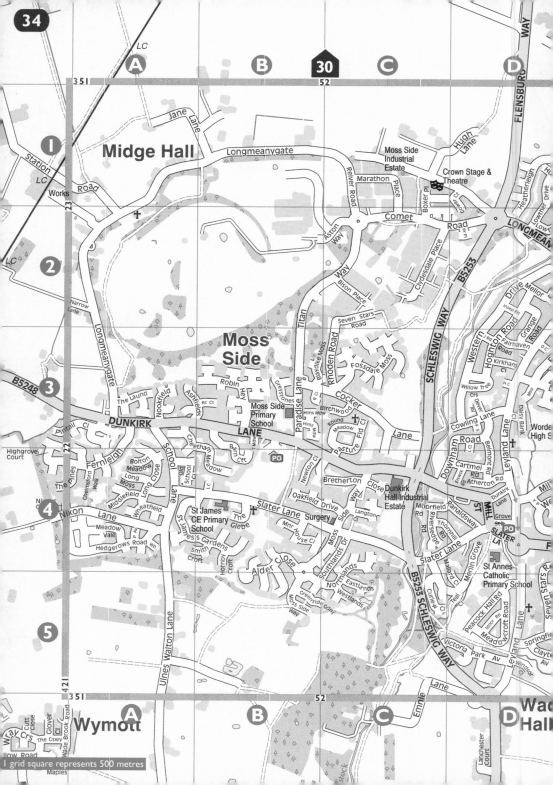

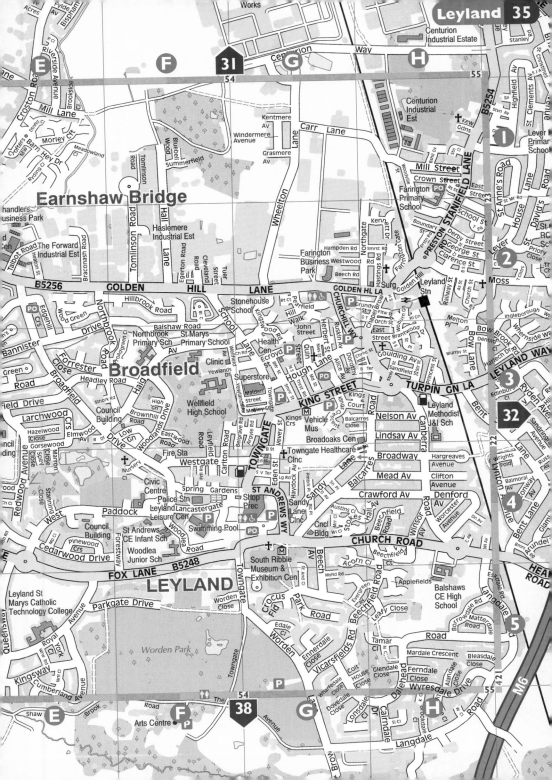

Camwood
Beech Tree
School
Clayton
Green Bus Park
Westwood
Prim Sch
Prim
Sch
Pines Close
Clayton Brook
Carr Field
Thorpe
Clayton Green
Sports Centre
WEST
B5256
Holt
E **F** Rd **33** 6 **G** **H**
Clayton Green
Hotel
58
Centre Dr
CLAYTON GREEN ROAD
PRESTON ROAD
A6
I Top
Lan
Cam Wood
Dovecote
B5256
HILL BROW
Glenmore
Sheep
Hill
Black
Croft
Kiln
Wood
The Clough
Manor
Croft
End
Pingle Croft
Lords Cft
Radburn Cl
Radburn Brow
PO
Pear Tree Rd
Mead Way
Bay Tree Lane
Sandy Lane
The Beeches
Barleyfield
Birch Field
Willow Rd
Ash
Team Meadow
Ashdown Drive
Osborne Drive
Chorley Old Road
59
23
2
Travelodge
Holly Cl
B Cft
Manor Road
Primary
School
Carr Road
Fiddler's Lane
Holly Cl
Oak croft
Stack Cft
Hill Croft
Clover Field
Hunts Field
Cedar
Field
Knbwrth
B Cl
Wilders wood Cl
Denham Lane
Blackthorn Cft
Whitethorn
Close
Lostock Meadow
Juniper Croft
Bearswood
Cft
Rowan Croft
Beech Gdns
Bankside Lane
Carlton Av
Back
Whittle Pk
Brownley St
The Elms
Swansey Lane
Derek Road
Wells Fold Close
St Helen's Rd
Birchin Lane
3
22
River Lostock
Woodside Av
A6
Watkin Road
Mill Lane
Hillside Crescent
Cliffe Drive
Smith Street
Hill Top Lane
4
Birchin Lane
Low
Cop
PRESTON ROAD
Kem
Mill Lane
Whittle Le Woods CE
Primary School
Cow Well Lane
Mount
Pleasant
Paradise Cl
Church Hill
Union
Crss
Carwood La
Keys Dr
Delph Way
Lisieux Hall
Hospital
Surgery
Langdale
Gv
Chorley Old Road
Grsm Cl
Whittle-Le-Woods
5
B5248
Shaw Hi Brow
A6
PO
Par Nook
Town Lane
Lady Crosse Drive
Town Lane
Leeds
59
421
E **F** **40** **G** **H**
Golf Course
Shaw Hill
Spinney Close
Shaw Hi Dr
PRESTON
Parkside Two Cft
Harvest Drive
Dunham Drive
Lucas Lane
**Johnson's
Hillock**
Shaw Hill
Hotel Golf &
Country Club
58

Back Lane

Works

WIGAN ROAD

A49

DAWSON LANE

Works

Works

Works

Works

Works

Shaw Brook Cl

Chestnut Av

Limes Av

Cedar

Wigan Rd

Milestone Mdw

Belfry Close

Chorley Business & Technology Cen

Grange Drive

Orchard Cl

Euxton Lane

Euxton Lane

Works

Woodcock Fold

Birkdale Cl

Wntw'th Dr

Turnbury

East Ter

Ml Stn Mdw

Avenue

Briar Avenue

Yew Tree Av

Poplar Av

Runshaw La

St Marys Ga

PO

Barnside

Woodside

Greenside

Orchard Cl

Sycamore Avenue

Works

Oak Av

Lane

School Lane

Pear Tree Lane

Whinny Lane

Washington Lane

Croffer's Gn

Village CPE

St Schl La

The Ferries

Old Schl

Vicarage

Euxton St Marys RC

Euxton CE Prim Sch

Brookside

Casterton

Earls Way

Park Av

Church Walk

Euxton Hall Gdns

Princess Way

Empress Way

Talbot Dr

Regents

Countess Way

Barons Wy

Way

Queensway

Kingsway

WEST WAY

A419

Long Copse

Long Copse

Merefield

The Farthing

Chanc

Thrilfil

Mundley

Euxton Hall Hospital

BALSHAW LANE

A581

PORT RD

B5252

FOXH

Euxton Balshaw Lane Stn

Anderton Rd

Dale

Highways Av

Chiltern Av

Coniston

Cotswold Cl

Conway Cl

Hawk

Mallom Av

nere Cl

Bredon Av

Balshaw Lane Primary School

Works

Leeds & Liverpool Canal

Meadow St
West St
VW
Stable Lane
Abt St
Victoria St
Millbrook Cl
Ryefield

Briers Brow

Wheelton

61
21

E
F
G
H

Copthurst Lane
Lane
Blackburn Road
60

St Chads RC Primary School

Town Lane

I

Dark Lane
Lane

Spring Mews

Tanhouse Lane

Spring Crs

Heapey

A674

Premier Lodge

Chapel Lane

2

BLACKBURN ROAD

20

Gorse Cl

B6228

Guildford Av
Epsom Close
Ewell Cl
Carleton
Dorking Road
Sutton Gv
Ealing
Reigate
Road
SBR
Reynill Gv
Melford Cl
A Rd
Merton Gv

Barn Lane

3

Tithe

Coppice Lane

A674

Merlin Close

Heapey Road
Kittiwake Road
The Dingle
The Wold
KCI
Osprey Close
Higher

4

419

18

Leeds and Liverpool Canal

Paradise St

High Bank
The Dell
Blackbrook Cl
Torthore Cl

House Lane

Morris Farm

Hollin

5

Blackburn Brow

Knowley Brow

Botany Brow

Bagganley Lane

M61

Northgate Dr
Ch Av
Larch
Daisy Fold
Mason St
St Peters CE Primary School

60
61

E
F
45
G
H

B6228
Smithills
Withnell
ville Rd
Nab Rd
orough
er's St
PO
Bagganley
Belmo
1 Dr
Coppice
Mont
Holcombe Gv
Dunscar Gv
Moorfields Gv
La

Healey Nab

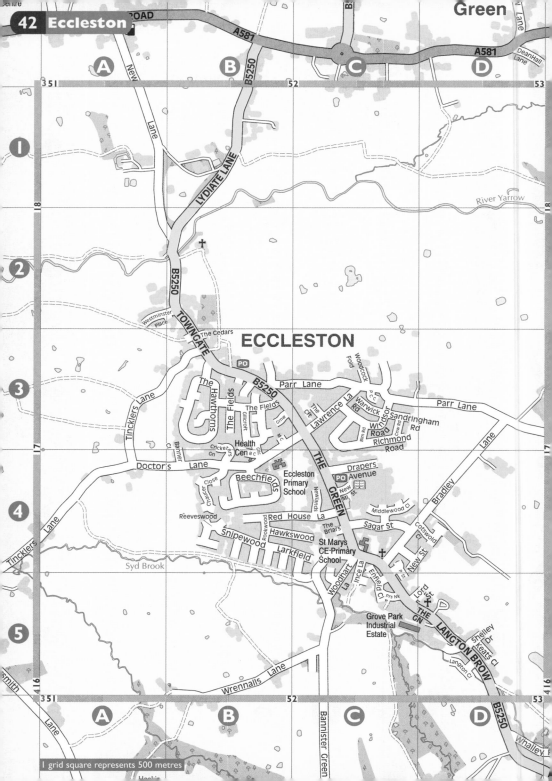

Green

A581

A581

DeanHall Lane

New Lane

LYDIATE LANE

B5250

River Yarrow

B5250

TOWNGATE

Westminster Place

The Cedars

ECCLESTON

PO

B5250

Parr Lane

Woodcock Fold

Parr Lane

The Hawthorns

The Fields

The Fields

Gillcroft

Lawrence La

Warwick Rd

Windsor Road

Sandringham Rd

Tincklers Lane

Cricket Gn

Health Cen

THE GREEN

Richmond Road

Doctor's Lane

Banner Cl

Chaucer

Close

Beechfields

Eccleston Primary School

Drapers Avenue

PO

New MI. St.

Reeveswood

Red House La

Newlands

Middlewood Cl

Bradley

Lane

Cotswold

Snipewood

Hawkswood

The Briars

Sagar St

Larkfield

St Marys CE Primary School

New St

Tincklers Lane

Syd Brook

Woodhart La

Ince La

Enfield Cl

Prs Nk

Lord Ct

THE GN

THE LANGTON BROW

Grove Park Industrial Estate

Shelley Dr

Keats Cl

Langton Cl

Wrennalls Lane

Bannister Green

B5250

Whalley

Lane

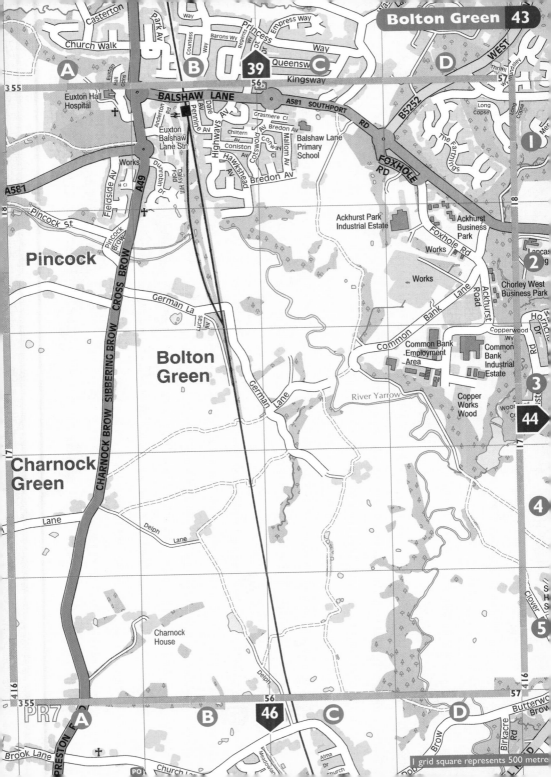

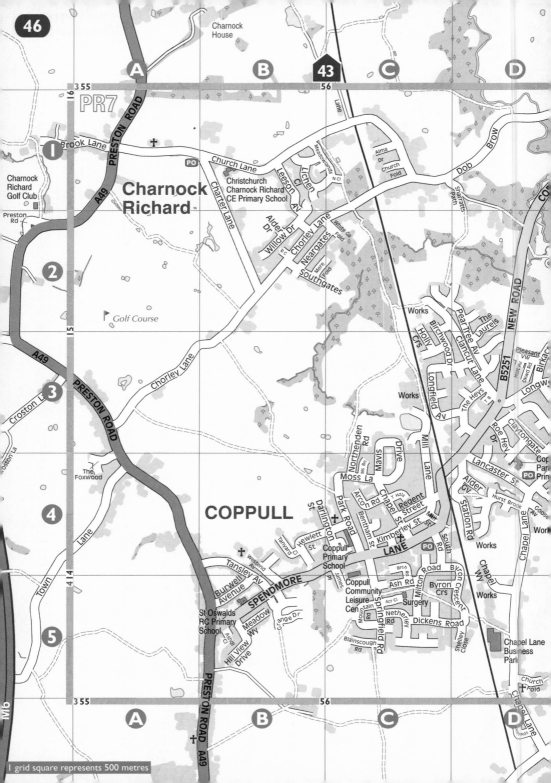

E

MOOR ROAD

F

44
58

G

Weld Bank

H

I

59
16

B5251

Lwr Burgh Way

The Copse

The Oaks

The Cedars

Lower Burgh Way

Burgh

Sevenoaks

Dale VW

The Willows

Stonyhurst

St Hilda's Cl

Holy Cross RC High School

Duxbury Park Golf Club

Chest Aven

Winchester Av

Duxbury Hall

River Yarrow

Lower Burgh Road

Birkacre

Burgh Hall

Burgh Hall Road

Capesthorne Dr

Saunders Ms

Woodlands Meadow

Yewtree

Firtree

Duxbury P Golf Course

2

Duxbury Jubilee Park Golf Club

15

3

WIGAN LANE

Sunny Brow

River Yarrow

South Lane

Burgh Lane

Grundy's Lane

4

414

Coppull Hall Lane

Old Hall

A5106

5

59
58

E

F

G

H

Coppull Hall Lane

Tar Lane

LANE

All Saints CE Primary School

Hodder Ca

Eaves Green Road

St Gregory's Pl

Gregorys holic nary Sch

Works

Saville S

Weld La

Carr La

kingsmead

Kirkstall

Berkeley Close

Carr Lane

Little Carr Lane

School

The Bowers

Bamber Bridge	25 F5	Eccleston	42 B3
Birkacre	47 E2	Euxton	38 D5
Blackleach	4 A3	Farington	31 E3
Bolton Green	43 B3	Farington Moss	30 C4
Broadfield	35 E3	Fishwick	19 E3
Brookfield	13 G4	Fulwood	12 B3
Broughton	6 D2	Grange	14 A4
Cadley	11 G4	Gregson Lane	27 E4
Catforth	4 B1	Grimsargh	9 H4
Charnock Richard	46 A1	Haighton Green	8 C3
Chorley	44 B1	Haighton Top	7 H4
Clayton Brook	33 E4	Hartwood	40 D5
Clayton Green	33 E5	Higher Bartle	5 G5
Clayton-le-Woods	36 B2	Higher Penwortham	23 G2
Coppull	46 B4	Higher Walton	26 C3
Cottam	10 C2	Holme Slack	13 F4
Coup Green	26 D2	Howick Cross	22 D2
Cow Hill	9 E4	Hutton	22 A4
Cowling	45 E4	Ingol	11 E4
Cuerden Green	32 A3	Johnson's Hillock	40 D1
Earnshaw Bridge	35 E1	Kingsfold	23 H5

Larches	16 D2	Pudding Pie Nook	1
Lea	16 B2	Red Scar	1
Leyland	31 E3	Ribbleton	1
Lightfoot Green	35 F5	Riversway Docklands	1
Limbrick	6 A4	Roach Bridge	2
Longridge	45 G5	Runshaw Moor	3
Longton	28 C2	Samlesbury	2
Lostock Hall	31 G2	Seed Lee	33
Lower Bartle	10 B1	Sharoe Green	12
Lower Penwortham	24 A1	Swillbrook	4
Lucas Green	40 B1	Tanterton	11
Middleforth Green	23 H2	Tardy Gate	31
Midge Hall	34 A1	Walmer Bridge	28
Moor Side	5 G1	Walton-le-Dale	24
Moss Side	34 B3	Walton Summit	26
New Longton	30 A1	Weld Bank	44
New Town	15 B5	White Stake	30
Nog Tow	10 D1	Whittle-le-Woods	37
Penwortham Lane	24 B4	Willacy Lane End	4
Pincock	43 A2	Woodplumpton	5
Preston	3 H4		

USING THE STREET INDEX

Street names are listed alphabetically. Each street name is followed by its postal town or area locality, the Postcode District, the page number, and the reference to the square in which the name is found.

Standard index entries are shown as follows:

Abbey St *FUL/RIB* PR2......................**2** B2

Street names and selected addresses not shown on the map due to scale restrictions are shown in the index with an asterisk:

Alexandra Pavilions *PRES* * PR1......**3** H1

GENERAL ABBREVIATIONS

ACC	ACCESS	E	EAST	LDG	LODGE	R	RIVE
ALY	ALLEY	EMB	EMBANKMENT	LGT	LIGHT	RBT	ROUNDABOU
AP	APPROACH	EMBY	EMBASSY	LK	LOCK	RD	ROA
AR	ARCADE	ESP	ESPLANADE	LKS	LOCKS	RDG	RIDG
ASS	ASSOCIATION	EST	ESTATE	LNDG	LANDING	REP	REPUBLI
AV	AVENUE	EX	EXCHANGE	LTL	LITTLE	RES	RESERVOI
BCH	BEACH	EXPY	EXPRESSWAY	LWR	LOWER	RFC	RUGBY FOOTBALL CLU
BLDS	BUILDINGS	EXT	EXTENSION	MAG	MAGISTRATE	RI	RIS
BND	BEND	F/O	FLYOVER	MAN	MANSIONS	RP	RAM
BNK	BANK	FC	FOOTBALL CLUB	MD	MEAD	RW	ROV
BR	BRIDGE	FK	FORK	MDW	MEADOW	S	SOUT
BRK	BROOK	FLD	FIELD	MEM	MEMORIAL	SCH	SCHOO
BTM	BOTTOM	FLDS	FIELDS	MKT	MARKET	SE	SOUTH EAS
BUS	BUSINESS	FLS	FALLS	MKTS	MARKETS	SER	SERVICE ARE
BVD	BOULEVARD	FLS	FLATS	ML	MALL	SH	SHOR
BY	BYPASS	FM	FARM	ML	MILL	SHOP	SHOPPIN
CATH	CATHEDRAL	FT	FORT	MNR	MANOR	SKWY	SKYWA
CEM	CEMETERY	FWY	FREEWAY	MS	MEWS	SMT	SUMMI
CEN	CENTRE	FY	FERRY	MSN	MISSION	SOC	SOCIET
CFT	CROFT	GA	GATE	MT	MOUNT	SP	SPUR
CH	CHURCH	GAL	GALLERY	MTN	MOUNTAIN	SPR	SPRINC
CHA	CHASE	GDN	GARDEN	MTS	MOUNTAINS	SQ	SQUARE
CHYD	CHURCHYARD	GDNS	GARDENS	MUS	MUSEUM	ST	STREET
CIR	CIRCLE	GLD	GLADE	MWY	MOTORWAY	STN	STATION
CIRC	CIRCUS	GLN	GLEN	N	NORTH	STR	STREAM
CL	CLOSE	GN	GREEN	NE	NORTH EAST	STRD	STRAND
CLFS	CLIFFS	GND	GROUND	NW	NORTH WEST	SW	SOUTH WEST
CMP	CAMP	GRA	GRANGE	O/P	OVERPASS	TDG	TRADING
CNR	CORNER	GRG	GARAGE	OFF	OFFICE	TER	TERRACE
CO	COUNTY	GT	GREAT	ORCH	ORCHARD	THWY	THROUGHWAY
COLL	COLLEGE	GTWY	GATEWAY	OV	OVAL	TNL	TUNNEL
COM	COMMON	GV	GROVE	PAL	PALACE	TOLL	TOLLWAY
COMM	COMMISSION	HGR	HIGHER	PAS	PASSAGE	TPK	TURNPIKE
CON	CONVENT	HL	HILL	PAV	PAVILION	TR	TRACK
COT	COTTAGE	HLS	HILLS	PDE	PARADE	TRL	TRAIL
COTS	COTTAGES	HO	HOUSE	PH	PUBLIC HOUSE	TWR	TOWER
CP	CAPE	HOL	HOLLOW	PK	PARK	U/P	UNDERPASS
CPS	COPSE	HOSP	HOSPITAL	PKWY	PARKWAY	UNI	UNIVERSITY
CR	CREEK	HRB	HARBOUR	PL	PLACE	UPR	UPPER
CREM	CREMATORIUM	HTH	HEATH	PLN	PLAIN	V	VALE
CRS	CRESCENT	HTS	HEIGHTS	PLNS	PLAINS	VA	VALLEY
CSWY	CAUSEWAY	HVN	HAVEN	PLZ	PLAZA	VIAD	VIADUCT
CT	COURT	HWY	HIGHWAY	POL	POLICE STATION	VIL	VILLA
CTRL	CENTRAL	IMP	IMPERIAL	PR	PRINCE	VIS	VISTA
CTS	COURTS	IN	INLET	PREC	PRECINCT	VLG	VILLAGE
CTYD	COURTYARD	IND EST	INDUSTRIAL ESTATE	PREP	PREPARATORY	VLS	VILLAS
CUTT	CUTTINGS	INF	INFIRMARY	PRIM	PRIMARY	VW	VIEW
CV	COVE	INFO	INFORMATION	PROM	PROMENADE	W	WEST
CYN	CANYON	INT	INTERCHANGE	PRS	PRINCESS	WD	WOOD
DEPT	DEPARTMENT	IS	ISLAND	PRT	PORT	WHF	WHARF
DL	DALE	JCT	JUNCTION	PT	POINT	WK	WALK
DM	DAM	JTY	JETTY	PTH	PATH	WKS	WALKS
DR	DRIVE	KG	KING	PZ	PIAZZA	WLS	WELLS
DRO	DROVE	KNL	KNOLL	QD	QUADRANT	WY	WAY
DRY	DRIVEWAY	L	LAKE	QU	QUEEN	YD	YARD
DWGS	DWELLINGS	LA	LANE	QY	QUAY	YHA	YOUTH HOSTEL

POSTCODE TOWNS AND AREA ABBREVIATIONS

BBR	Bamber Bridge	CHLYE	Chorley east/Adlington/	FUL/RIB	Fulwood/Ribbleton	LEYL	Leyland
BRSC	Burscough		Whittle-le-Woods	GAR/LONG	Garstang/Longridge	PRES	Preston
CHLY/EC	Chorley/Eccleston	CROS/BRETH	Croston/Bretherton	KIRK/FR/WAR	Kirkham/Freckleton/Warton		

A

y St FUL/RIB PR2.....2 B2
y Wk PRES PR1.....23 H4
t Meadow PRES PR1.....23 H2
tsway PRES PR1.....23 G1
tt Cft KIRK/FR/WA PR4.....11 E1
gdon Dr FUL/RIB PR2.....17 E2
a Rd FUL/RIB PR2.....19 G1
Gv FUL/RIB PR2.....13 H5
urst Rd CHLY/EC PR7.....43 D2
field BER PR5.....33 G5
gate La PRES PR1.....19 F2
swood Cl CHLY/EC PR7.....46 C5
aide St CHLY/EC PR7.....3 K3
phi Pl PRES PR1.....2 E2
phi St PRES PR1.....2 D1
iral Wy FUL/RIB PR2.....16 B3
s St PRES PR1.....3 G2
dale Dr FUL/RIB PR2.....16 C1
ie Rd FUL/RIB PR2.....12 A5
dale Cl LEYL PR25.....35 H5
ny Ct CHLYE PR6.....45 E2
ny Dr BER PR5.....25 F4
cros St PRES PR1.....18 D1
rt Rd FUL/RIB PR2.....12 B4
/L PR25.....18 A3
ES PR1.....18 B1
rt St CHLY/EC PR7.....44 D5
rt Ter PRES PR1.....3 H1
n St CHLY/EC PR7.....44 C3
ghton Cl BER PR5.....31 H2
ghton Crs BER PR5.....31 H2
ghton Rd BER PR5.....31 G2
n Bank Rd PRES PR1.....3 J4
n St East PRES PR1.....3 K4
ster Av PRES PR1.....23 G1
te Gv FUL/RIB PR2.....17 E1
iffe Rd FUL/RIB PR2.....16 C2
r Cl CROS/BRETH PR26.....34 B5
r Coppice FUL/RIB PR2.....10 C5
r Dr BER PR5.....26 D5
LY/EC PR7.....46 B2
rfield PRES PR1.....23 H3
r Gv CHLY/EC PR7.....46 D4
r Rd FUL/RIB PR2.....14 A4
rsleigh Crs BER PR5.....26 D5
ander Rd FUL/RIB PR2.....9 H4
andra Pavilions PRES * PR1.....3 H1
andra Rd BER PR5.....25 E3
R/LONG PR3.....15 B3
andra St PRES PR1.....19 E4
rd Fold FUL/RIB PR2.....11 H1
Av LEYL PR25.....35 G3
Sq PRES PR1.....3 H1
La CHLYE PR6.....40 A4
r St CHLY/EC PR7.....44 C3
aby Av FUL/RIB PR2.....12 C4
gate FUL/RIB PR2.....12 B4
ton Rd BER PR5.....25 F3
gton Cl BER PR5.....25 G3
a Dr CHLY/EC PR7.....46 C1
a Rw BER PR5.....27 E5
a St PRES PR1.....3 G1
ond Cl FUL/RIB PR2.....13 E2
ES PR1.....23 F3
e Cl BER PR5.....31 H2
e Cl BER PR5.....31 H2
e Rd CHLYE PR6.....41 E4
p St PRES PR1.....18 A1
n St PRES PR1.....19 F2
rn Av FUL/RIB PR2.....11 H4
rn Crs FUL/RIB PR2.....11 H4
er Dr CHLYE PR6.....45 E4
er Ga FUL/RIB PR2.....10 D2
ledene BER PR5.....33 E4
leside Av CHLY/EC * PR7.....43 B1
leside Cl BER PR5.....25 G4
leside Rd FUL/RIB PR2.....13 G3
leway BER PR5.....25 F2
rose Hall La
RK/FR/WA PR4.....5 G2
rose St LEYL PR25.....35 H2
rsham Cl KIRK/FR/WA PR4.....29 D1
leforth Dr BER PR5.....24 C5
or Cl PRES PR1.....3 F4
nor Dr KIRK/FR/WA PR4.....22 B4
erton Rd CHLY/EC PR7.....43 B1
erton St CHLY/EC PR7.....44 C1
ertons Wy FUL/RIB PR2.....13 E3

Andrew St PRES PR1.....19 E2
Aniline St CHLYE PR6.....45 E2
Annis St PRES PR1.....19 E3
Ansdell Gv FUL/RIB PR2.....11 G5
Ansdell St PRES * PR1.....19 E1
Appleby Cl BER PR5.....27 E5
Applefields LEYL PR25.....35 H5
Applesike KIRK/FR/WA PR4.....28 B2
Appletree Cl PRES PR1.....23 F4
Apsley Fold GAR/LONG * PR3.....15 C4
Aqueduct St PRES PR1.....2 B1
Arcon Rd CHLY/EC PR7.....46 C4
Ardee Rd PRES PR1.....2 B7
Argyle Rd LEYL PR25.....35 G4
Argyll Rd PRES PR1.....18 C2
Arkholme Dr KIRK/FR/WA PR4.....28 B1
Arkwright Rd PRES PR1.....18 B1
Arley St CHLY/EC PR7.....44 D2
Armstrong St FUL/RIB PR2.....17 F1
Arndale Rd GAR/LONG PR3.....15 B3
Arnhem Rd PRES PR1.....19 F3
Arnold Cl FUL/RIB PR2.....19 C1
Arnold Pl CHLY/EC PR7.....44 A5
Arno St PRES PR1.....3 J5
Arnott Rd CHLY/EC PR7.....17 G1
Arnside Cl BER PR5.....27 E2
Arnside Rd FUL/RIB PR2.....16 C1
Arrowsmith St BER PR5.....27 E4
Arrowsmith Dr BER PR5.....27 E4
Arroyo Wy FUL/RIB PR2.....12 D4
Arthur St PRES PR1.....2 D4
Arundel Pl PRES PR1.....3 H5
Arundel Rd KIRK/FR/WA PR4.....28 C1
Arundel Wy LEYL PR25.....36 A4
Ashbourne Crs FUL/RIB PR2.....11 E5
Ashby St CHLY/EC PR7.....44 C4
Ash Coppice FUL/RIB PR2.....10 B5
Ashdale Cl CHLY/EC PR7.....46 B5
Ashdown Dr CHLYE PR6.....37 G1
Ashdown Ms FUL/RIB PR2.....13 G2
Ashdown St PRES PR1.....19 F2
Ashfield FUL/RIB PR2.....10 D2
Ashfield Rd CHLY/EC PR7.....44 C5
Ashfields CROS/BRETH PR26.....34 A3
Ashford Crs GAR/LONG PR3.....6 C4
Ashford Rd FUL/RIB PR2.....16 C1
Ash Gv BER PR5.....24 C5
CHLY/EC PR7.....44 C5
KIRK/FR/WA PR4.....28 B2
KIRK/FR/WA PR4.....29 D3
Ashgrove PRES PR1.....19 F2
Ash Holme PRES PR1.....13 E5
Ash La GAR/LONG PR3.....15 C2
Ashleigh Ct FUL/RIB PR2.....12 C1
Ashleigh St PRES PR1.....19 E4
Ash Meadow FUL/RIB PR2.....10 C5
Ashmoor St PRES PR1.....2 D1
Ashness Cl FUL/RIB PR2.....7 F5
Ash Rd CHLY/EC PR7.....46 C5
Ashton Cl FUL/RIB PR2.....17 E2
Ashtongate FUL/RIB PR2.....16 C2
Ashton St FUL/RIB PR2.....2 C3
GAR/LONG PR3.....15 B2
Ashtree Ct BER PR5.....26 C3
Ashtree Gv PRES PR1.....23 F2
Ashurst Rd LEYL PR25.....36 B3
Ashwood Rd FUL/RIB PR2.....11 H1
Ashworth Cl PRES PR1.....3 K7
Ashworth Gv PRES PR1.....19 E5
Ashworth La PRES PR1.....3 K7
Ashworth St BER PR5.....25 H4
PRES PR1.....3 H1
Asland Cl BER PR5.....32 D1
Aspden St BER PR5.....25 G5
The Aspels PRES PR1.....23 G2
Aspels Crs PRES PR1.....23 G2
Aspels Nook PRES PR1.....23 G2
Aspendale Cl KIRK/FR/WA PR4.....28 B1
Aspen Gdns CHLY/EC PR7.....44 B4
Aspinall Cl PRES PR1.....23 H4
Assheton Pl FUL/RIB PR2.....13 G4
Astley Rd CHLY/EC PR7.....44 B1
Astley St CHLY/EC PR7.....44 C3
GAR/LONG PR3.....15 B3
Aston Wy CROS/BRETH PR26.....34 C2
Athelstan Fold FUL/RIB PR2.....11 G5
Atherton Rd LEYL PR25.....34 D4
Athol Gv CHLYE PR6.....45 E4
Atholl St PRES PR1.....2 B3
Atkinson Cl PRES PR1.....3 F4
Aubigny Dr FUL/RIB PR2.....11 H4
Aughton Wk PRES PR1.....3 F1
Austin Crs FUL/RIB PR2.....11 F4
Austins Cl LEYL PR25.....35 G4
Avalwood Av KIRK/FR/WA PR4.....28 D2

Avenham Colonnade PRES PR1.....3 G6
Avenham La PRES PR1.....3 G5
Avenham Pl PRES * PR1.....3 H6
Avenham Rd CHLY/EC PR7.....44 C3
PRES PR1.....3 G5
Avenham St PRES PR1.....3 G4
Avenham Ter PRES PR1.....3 H6
The Avenue FUL/RIB PR2.....11 E2
FUL/RIB PR2.....16 B2
LEYL PR25.....38 B1
PRES PR1.....23 F1
Avon Br FUL/RIB PR2.....6 C5
Avondale Dr BER PR5.....31 H1
Avondale Rd CHLY/EC PR7.....44 C3
Avon Gdns KIRK/FR/WA PR4.....10 B3
Aysgarth Av FUL/RIB PR2.....12 B1
Azalea Cl FUL/RIB PR2.....13 E2
LEYL PR25.....36 C1

B

Back Ashby St CHLY/EC PR7.....44 C4
Back Bourne's Rw BER PR5.....27 E5
Back Club St BER PR5.....32 C2
Back Grimshaw St PRES PR1.....3 H4
Back La CHLYE PR6.....37 F2
KIRK/FR/WA PR4.....28 A2
LEYL PR25.....36 A5
Back Mt CHLY/EC * PR7.....44 C2
Back Seed St PRES * PR1.....2 E3
Back Starkie St PRES PR1.....3 F6
The Backs GAR/LONG PR3.....15 B4
Badgers Cft FUL/RIB PR2.....19 H2
Badgers Wk CHLY/EC PR7.....44 C1
Badgers Wy BER PR5.....24 D3
Bagganley La CHLYE PR6.....41 E5
Bagnold Rd PRES PR1.....19 F2
Bairstow St PRES PR1.....3 F5
Baker St LEYL PR25.....35 H2
Balcarres Cl LEYL PR25.....35 G4
Balcarres Pl LEYL PR25.....35 G3
Balcarres Rd CHLY/EC PR7.....44 C5
FUL/RIB PR2.....11 G5
LEYL PR25.....35 G3
Balderstone Rd PRES PR1.....23 H1
Baldwin St BER PR5.....32 C1
Balfour Rd FUL/RIB PR2.....12 A5
Balfour St LEYL PR25.....35 G3
Ballam Rd FUL/RIB PR2.....16 C2
Balmoral Av LEYL PR25.....36 A4
Balmoral Rd BER PR5.....25 F3
CHLY/EC PR7.....42 C3
CHLY/EC PR7.....44 B3
KIRK/FR/WA PR4.....28 B5
Balniel Cl CHLY/EC PR7.....44 B1
Balshaw Crs LEYL PR25.....35 G4
Balshaw La CHLY/EC PR7.....43 B1
Balshaw Rd LEYL PR25.....35 F5
Balshaw St BER * PR5.....25 G4
Bamber St CHLY/EC PR7.....44 B5
Banastre CHLY/EC PR7.....40 A5
Banbury Dr FUL/RIB PR2.....12 A4
Bank Cl KIRK/FR/WA PR4.....28 C2
Bank Cft KIRK/FR/WA PR4.....28 C2
Bank Head La BER PR5.....25 H4
Bank Pde PRES PR1.....3 G6
PRES PR1.....23 H3
Bank Pl FUL/RIB PR2.....17 C2
Banksfield Av FUL/RIB PR2.....11 G5
Banksfield Pl BER PR5.....32 D2
Bankside CHLYE PR6.....37 F3
Banks Rd FUL/RIB PR2.....11 G5
Bank St CHLY/EC PR7.....44 C2
Banner St CHLY/EC PR7.....42 B3
Bannerman Ter CHLYE PR6.....40 D5
Bannister Cl BER PR5.....26 B2
Bannister Dr LEYL PR25.....35 E3
Bannister Hall Crs BER PR5.....26 B2
Bannister Hall Dr BER PR5.....26 B2
Bannister Hall La BER PR5.....26 B2
Bannister La CROS/BRETH PR26.....30 D5
Bannister's Bit PRES PR1.....23 G4
Bannister St CHLY/EC PR7.....44 C3
Barclay Rd GAR/LONG PR3.....15 B3
Barden Fl FUL/RIB PR2.....13 H4
Bardsea Pl FUL/RIB PR2.....10 D5
Barleyfield CHLYE PR6.....37 G1
Barlow St PRES PR1.....18 A2
Barnacre Cl FUL/RIB PR2.....7 G5
Barnacre Rd GAR/LONG PR3.....15 B2
Barn Cft CROS/BRETH PR26.....34 B3
PRES PR1.....23 F2
Barnfield BER PR5.....31 G1
Barn Hey KIRK/FR/WA PR4.....28 C1
Barn Hey Dr CROS/BRETH PR26.....35 D1
Barn Meadow BER PR5.....33 F3

Barnsfold FUL/RIB PR2.....11 H2
Barnside CHLY/EC PR7.....39 E4
Barons Great Outdoors
CHLY/EC * PR7.....46 D5
Barons Wy CHLY/EC PR7.....39 F5
Barry Av FUL/RIB PR2.....10 D5
Bartle La KIRK/FR/WA PR4.....10 A1
Bartle Pl FUL/RIB PR2.....16 C2
Bashall Gv LEYL PR25.....35 H1
Basil St PRES PR1.....19 E1
Bath St FUL/RIB * PR2.....2 A1
Bayliss Cl FUL/RIB PR2.....13 H5
Bay Rd FUL/RIB PR2.....19 G1
Baytree Cl BER PR5.....32 A1
Bay Tree Farm FUL/RIB * PR2.....16 B3
Bay Tree Rd CHLYE PR6.....37 F2
Beachley Rd FUL/RIB PR2.....10 D4
Beacon Av FUL/RIB PR2.....11 H4
Beacon Gv FUL/RIB PR2.....11 H4
Beaconsfield Av PRES PR1.....19 H2
Beaconsfield Ter CHLYE PR6.....40 D5
Beacon St CHLY/EC PR7.....44 D3
Beamont Dr PRES PR1.....2 A2
Bearswood Cft CHLYE PR6.....37 F2
Beatty Av CHLY/EC PR7.....44 B4
Beaumaris Rd LEYL PR25.....36 A4
Beckett Ct PRES PR1.....3 F1
Bedford Rd FUL/RIB PR2.....12 C4
Beech Av CHLY/EC PR7.....38 D4
LEYL PR25.....35 G4
Beech Dr FUL/RIB PR2.....6 D5
GAR/LONG PR3.....15 B3
The Beeches CHLYE PR6.....37 G1
Beechfield Ct LEYL PR25.....35 H4
Beechfield Rd LEYL PR25.....35 G5
Beechfields CHLY/EC PR7.....42 B4
Beech Gdns CHLYE PR6.....37 F3
Beech Gv FUL/RIB PR2.....17 F2
Beech Hill Cl BER PR5.....25 G3
Beech Rd LEYL PR25.....35 G2
Beech St PRES PR1.....2 B6
Beech St South PRES PR1.....2 C7
Beech Ter PRES PR1.....2 C7
Beechway FUL/RIB * PR2.....12 C4
PRES PR1.....23 F3
Beechwood Av BER PR5.....25 E2
FUL/RIB PR2.....11 G4
Beechwood Cl CHLY/EC * PR7.....46 D5
Beechwood Cft CHLYE PR6.....37 E1
Bee La PRES PR1.....23 H5
Beenland St PRES PR1.....19 F2
Belfry Cl CHLYE PR6.....39 F3
Belgrave Av PRES PR1.....23 F3
Belgrave Ct FUL/RIB * PR2.....12 D1
Belgrave Rd LEYL PR25.....35 G4
Bellflower Cl LEYL PR25.....36 C1
Bellis Wy BER PR5.....24 D4
Bells La BER PR5.....27 E4
Belmont Av FUL/RIB PR2.....13 F5
Belmont Cl FUL/RIB PR2.....19 F1
Belmont Ct GAR/LONG PR3.....15 C3
Belmont Crs FUL/RIB PR2.....19 F1
Belmont Dr CHLYE PR6.....45 E1
Belmont Rd FUL/RIB PR2.....17 G1
LEYL PR25.....34 D3
Belton Hl FUL/RIB PR2.....6 D5
Belvedere Dr CHLY/EC PR7.....44 B2
Belvedere Rd LEYL * PR25.....35 H2
Bence Rd PRES PR1.....3 K5
Bengal St CHLY/EC PR7.....44 C1
Benson La KIRK/FR/WA PR4.....4 A2
Bentham St CHLY/EC PR7.....46 C4
Bent La LEYL PR25.....35 H3
Bentley Mnr FUL/RIB * PR2.....19 H1
Bentley Park Rd
KIRK/FR/WA PR4.....28 B3
Benton Rd FUL/RIB PR2.....13 F4
Berkeley Cl CHLY/EC PR7.....44 D5
Berkeley Dr BER PR5.....32 C5
Berkeley St PRES PR1.....18 A2
Berry Fld PRES PR1.....23 G3
Berry La GAR/LONG PR3.....15 B2
Berry St BER PR5.....31 G1
PRES PR1.....3 H5
Berwick Dr FUL/RIB PR2.....11 H4
Berwick Rd PRES PR1.....3 G5
Berwick St PRES * PR1.....19 G2
Beverley Cl FUL/RIB PR2.....17 G2
Bexhill Rd FUL/RIB PR2.....11 E5
Bhailok St PRES PR1.....2 D2
Bidston St PRES PR1.....19 G3
Bilsborough Hey PRES PR1.....24 A5
Bilsborough Meadow
FUL/RIB PR2.....10 C5
Binbrook Pl CHLY/EC PR7.....44 A2
Bingley Cl CHLYE PR6.....37 G2
Birch Av CHLY/EC PR7.....39 E3
FUL/RIB PR2.....17 E1

LEYL PR25 ... 36 C1
PRES PR1 ... 23 E3
Birch Crs *BER* PR5 ... 27 E5
Birch Fld *CHLYE* PR6 ... 37 F1
Birchfield Dr *GAR/LONG* PR3 ... 15 B2
Birchin La *CHLYE* PR6 ... 37 H3
Birchover Cl *FUL/RIB* PR2 ... 11 E3
Birch Rd *CHLY/EC* PR7 ... 46 C4
　CHLYE PR6 ... 40 D5
Birchwood *CROS/BRETH* PR26 ... 34 B3
Birchwood Av *KIRK/FR/WA* PR4 ... 28 D1
Birchwood Dr *FUL/RIB* PR2 ... 46 C2
　FUL/RIB PR2 ... 11 H1
Bird St *PRES* PR1 ... 2 B7
Birkacre Brow *CHLY/EC* PR7 ... 46 D1
Birkacre Rd *CHLY/EC* PR7 ... 46 D1
Birkdale Av *KIRK/FR/WA* PR4 ... 28 B2
Birkdale Cl *CHLYE* PR6 ... 39 F3
　KIRK/FR/WA PR4 ... 28 B2
Birkdale Dr *FUL/RIB* PR2 ... 16 C1
Birkett Dr *FUL/RIB* PR2 ... 14 A5
Birkett Pl *FUL/RIB* PR2 ... 14 A5
Birk St *PRES* PR1 ... 2 C4
Birley Bank *PRES* PR1 ... 19 E4
Birley St *PRES* PR1 ... 3 F3
Birtwistle St *BER* PR5 ... 31 H2
Bishopgate *PRES* PR1 ... 3 G3
Bishopsway *PRES* PR1 ... 23 H3
Bison Pl *CROS/BRETH* PR26 ... 34 C2
Bispham Av *CROS/BRETH* PR26 ... 31 E5
Bispham St *PRES* * PR1 ... 3 F2
Blackberry Wy *PRES* PR1 ... 23 F4
Blackbrook Cl *FUL/RIB* PR2 ... 41 G5
Black Bull La *FUL/RIB* PR2 ... 11 H4
Blackburn Brow *CHLYE* PR6 ... 41 G5
Blackburn Rd *BER* PR5 ... 26 B2
　CHLYE PR6 ... 41 G2
　GAR/LONG PR3 ... 15 D3
Blackburn St *CHLYE* PR6 ... 44 D3
Black Cft *CHLYE* PR6 ... 37 F1
Black Horse St *CHLY/EC* * PR7 ... 44 B4
Blackhurst Av *KIRK/FR/WA* PR4 ... 22 D4
Blackhurst St *FUL/RIB* PR2 ... 9 H4
Blackleach Av *KIRK/FR/WA* PR4 ... 4 B3
Blackpool Rd *FUL/RIB* PR2 ... 16 C3
　GAR/LONG PR3 ... 15 B3
　PRES PR1 ... 12 C5
Blackstone Rd *CHLYE* PR6 ... 45 E1
Blackthorn Cl *FUL/RIB* PR2 ... 16 B3
Blackthorn Cft *CHLYE* PR6 ... 37 E2
Blackthorn Dr *PRES* PR1 ... 23 F3
Blainscough Rd *CHLY/EC* PR7 ... 46 C5
Blake Av *BER* PR5 ... 31 G4
Blanche St *FUL/RIB* * PR2 ... 17 G2
Blashaw La *PRES* PR1 ... 23 E1
Blaydike Moss *CROS/BRETH* PR26 ... 34 B3
Bleachers Dr *LEYL* PR25 ... 35 E3
Bleasdale Cl *BER* PR5 ... 32 D1
　LEYL PR25 ... 35 H5
Bleasdale St East *PRES* PR1 ... 3 K1
Blelock St *PRES* PR1 ... 3 F3
Blenheim Cl *BER* PR5 ... 32 A1
Blenheim Wy *KIRK/FR/WA* PR4 ... 10 C2
Bloomfield Ct *PRES* PR1 ... 18 A1
Bloomfield Gra *PRES* PR1 ... 23 G4
The Blossoms *FUL/RIB* PR2 ... 13 E2
Bluebell Cl *CHLYE* PR6 ... 40 B2
Blue Bell Pl *PRES* PR1 ... 3 H3
Bluebell Wy *BER* PR5 ... 33 E1
　FUL/RIB PR2 ... 13 G2
Bluebell Wd *LEYL* PR25 ... 35 F1
Blundell La *PRES* PR1 ... 17 F5
Blundell Rd *FUL/RIB* PR2 ... 12 A5
Boarded Barn *CHLY/EC* PR7 ... 39 E4
Bodmin St *PRES* PR1 ... 19 F2
Boegrave Av *BER* PR5 ... 31 G1
Bold St *PRES* PR1 ... 17 H1
Bolton Meadow *CROS/BRETH* PR26 ... 34 A4
Bolton Rd *CHLY/EC* PR7 ... 44 D4
Boltons Ct *PRES* PR1 ... 3 G4
Bolton St *CHLY/EC* PR7 ... 44 C3
Bone Cft *CHLYE* PR6 ... 37 F3
Bootle St *PRES* PR1 ... 19 E2
Borrowdale Rd *LEYL* PR25 ... 35 H5
Bostock St *PRES* * PR1 ... 3 G4
Botany Brow *CHLYE* PR6 ... 41 E5
Boulevard *PRES* PR1 ... 24 D1
Boundary Cl *CHLY/EC* PR7 ... 42 B4
　KIRK/FR/WA PR4 ... 29 D1
Boundary Rd *FUL/RIB* PR2 ... 11 H5
Boundary St *LEYL* PR25 ... 35 H2
Bournesfield *BER* PR5 ... 27 E5
Bourne's Rw *BER* PR5 ... 27 E5
Bow Brook Rd *LEYL* PR25 ... 35 H3

The Bowers *CHLY/EC* PR7 ... 47 H1
Bowland Av *CHLYE* PR6 ... 44 D2
Bowland Cl *GAR/LONG* PR3 ... 15 C2
Bowland Pl *FUL/RIB* PR2 ... 14 A5
Bowland Rd *FUL/RIB* PR2 ... 14 A5
Bow La *LEYL* PR25 ... 35 H3
　PRES PR1 ... 2 C4
Bowlers Cl *FUL/RIB* PR2 ... 13 E3
Bowlingfield *FUL/RIB* PR2 ... 11 E2
Bowness Rd *PRES* PR1 ... 20 A2
Bowran St *PRES* PR1 ... 2 E3
Bow St *LEYL* PR25 ... 35 H2
Boxer Pl *CROS/BRETH* PR26 ... 34 C2
Boys La *FUL/RIB* PR2 ... 11 G3
Brabiner La *FUL/RIB* PR2 ... 9 F2
Bracewell Rd *FUL/RIB* PR2 ... 13 G3
Brackenbury Cl *BER* PR5 ... 31 G2
Brackenbury Rd *PRES* PR1 ... 12 A5
Brackenbury St *PRES* PR1 ... 18 B1
Bracken Cl *CHLYE* PR6 ... 45 E3
Braconash Rd *LEYL* PR25 ... 35 E2
Braddon St *PRES* PR1 ... 19 F2
Bradkirk La *BER* PR5 ... 33 F1
Bradkirk Pl *BER* PR5 ... 33 E2
Bradley La *CHLY/EC* PR7 ... 42 D4
Braefield Crs *FUL/RIB* PR2 ... 13 H5
Braintree Av *PRES* PR1 ... 24 A4
Bramble Ct *PRES* PR1 ... 24 A4
The Brambles *CHLY/EC* PR7 ... 46 D3
　FUL/RIB PR2 ... 13 F2
Brampton St *FUL/RIB* PR2 ... 17 G2
Brancker St *CHLY/EC* PR7 ... 44 A5
Brandiforth St *BER* PR5 ... 25 G4
Brandwood *PRES* PR1 ... 23 E2
Brant Rd *PRES* PR1 ... 20 A2
Brantwood Dr *LEYL* PR25 ... 35 H3
Bray St *FUL/RIB* * PR2 ... 17 G3
Bredon Av *CHLY/EC* PR7 ... 43 C1
Breeze Mt *BER* PR5 ... 32 A2
Brennand St *BER* PR5 ... 32 D1
Bretherton Cl *CROS/BRETH* PR26 ... 34 C4
Bretherton Ter *LEYL* PR25 ... 35 G3
Brewery St *GAR/LONG* PR3 ... 15 C3
Briar Av *CHLY/EC* PR7 ... 39 E3
Briar Bank Rw *FUL/RIB* PR2 ... 7 F5
Briar Cft *KIRK/FR/WA* PR4 ... 28 C3
Briar Gv *FUL/RIB* PR2 ... 11 E4
The Briars *CHLY/EC* PR7 ... 42 C4
　FUL/RIB PR2 ... 13 F2
Briarwood Cl *LEYL* PR25 ... 34 D4
Bridge Bank *BER* PR5 ... 19 E5
Bridge End *BER* PR5 ... 31 G1
Bridge Rd *BER* PR5 ... 32 A1
　FUL/RIB PR2 ... 17 G1
Bridge St *BER* PR5 ... 26 B3
　BER PR5 ... 32 C2
Bridge Ter *BER* * PR5 ... 19 E5
Bridgeway *BER* PR5 ... 32 A1
Briercliffe Rd *CHLYE* PR6 ... 44 D1
Brierfield *KIRK/FR/WA* PR4 ... 29 D1
Brierley Rd *BER* PR5 ... 33 E2
Brierley St *PRES* PR1 ... 17 H2
Briery Cl *FUL/RIB* PR2 ... 13 E4
Brieryfield Rd *PRES* PR1 ... 2 B3
Briery Hey *BER* PR5 ... 33 F5
Briggs Rd *FUL/RIB* PR2 ... 17 G1
Brighton Crs *FUL/RIB* PR2 ... 11 E5
Brighton St *CHLYE* * PR6 ... 45 E2
Brindle Cl *BER* PR5 ... 31 G3
　GAR/LONG PR3 ... 15 C3
Brindle Fold *BER* PR5 ... 33 G2
Brindle Rd *BER* PR5 ... 25 H4
　CHLYE PR6 ... 33 H3
Brindle St *CHLY/EC* PR7 ... 44 C4
　PRES PR1 ... 19 E3
Bristol Av *LEYL* PR25 ... 32 A5
Bristow Av *FUL/RIB* PR2 ... 17 F1
Britannia Dr *FUL/RIB* PR2 ... 17 F3
Brixey St *PRES* PR1 ... 2 B7
Brixton Rd *PRES* PR1 ... 3 K5
Broad Cft *KIRK/FR/WA* PR4 ... 28 C1
Broadfield *KIRK/FR/WA* PR4 ... 6 B3
Broadfield Dr *LEYL* PR25 ... 35 E3
　PRES PR1 ... 23 H4
Broadfields *CHLY/EC* PR7 ... 40 B5
Broadgate *PRES* PR1 ... 2 B7
Broadgreen Cl *LEYL* PR25 ... 35 F3
Broad Meadow *BER* PR5 ... 31 G1
Broad Oak Gn *PRES* PR1 ... 23 H3
Broad Oak La *KIRK/FR/WA* PR4 ... 23 F4
Broad Sq *LEYL* PR25 ... 35 G4
Broad St *LEYL* PR25 ... 35 G4
Broadway *FUL/RIB* PR2 ... 11 H2
　FUL/RIB PR2 ... 16 D1
　LEYL PR25 ... 35 H4
Broadwood Cl *PRES* PR1 ... 23 F2

Broadwood Dr *FUL/RIB* PR2 ... 12 A1
Brockholes Brow *PRES* PR1 ... 19 H2
Brockholes Vw *PRES* PR1 ... 19 E4
Brock Rd *CHLYE* PR6 ... 44 D1
Bromley Gn *CHLYE* PR6 ... 41 F3
Bromley St *PRES* * PR1 ... 2 B2
Brook Cft *FUL/RIB* PR2 ... 11 F5
Brookdale *KIRK/FR/WA* PR4 ... 30 A3
Brookdale Cl *LEYL* PR25 ... 38 D1
Brooke St *CHLYE* PR6 ... 44 D3
Brookfield Av *FUL/RIB* PR2 ... 13 E4
Brookfield Dr *FUL/RIB* PR2 ... 7 E5
Brookfield Pl *BER* PR5 ... 33 E3
Brookfield St *PRES* PR1 ... 18 B2
Brook Hey *KIRK/FR/WA* PR4 ... 28 B2
Brookhouse Cl *BER* PR5 ... 27 F4
Brookhouse Dr *BER* PR5 ... 27 F4
Brookhouse St *FUL/RIB* PR2 ... 17 H2
Brooklands *FUL/RIB* PR2 ... 17 G2
Brooklands Av *FUL/RIB* PR2 ... 12 A1
Brook La *CROS/BRETH* PR26 ... 30 D3
Brook Meadow
　KIRK/FR/WA PR4 ... 10 D2
Brook Pl *FUL/RIB* PR2 ... 16 B1
Brook Rd North *FUL/RIB* PR2 ... 11 H5
Brookside *CHLY/EC* PR7 ... 39 E5
　CHLY/EC PR7 ... 46 D4
Brookside Cl *CROS/BRETH* PR26 ... 35 E1
Brookside Rd *FUL/RIB* PR2 ... 11 H1
Brook St *BER* PR5 ... 26 B3
　FUL/RIB PR2 ... 11 H5
Brookview *FUL/RIB* PR2 ... 12 D5
Brookway *KIRK/FR/WA* PR4 ... 28 B2
Broom Cl *LEYL* PR25 ... 36 C1
Broomfield Mill St *PRES* PR1 ... 18 B2
Broughton St *PRES* PR1 ... 12 A5
Broughton Tower Wy
　FUL/RIB PR2 ... 7 G5
Brow Hey *BER* PR5 ... 33 F3
Brownedge Cl *BER* PR5 ... 25 F5
Brownedge La *BER* PR5 ... 25 G5
Brownedge Rd *BER* PR5 ... 25 F5
Brownhill La *KIRK/FR/WA* PR4 ... 29 D5
Brownhill Rd *LEYL* PR25 ... 35 F3
Browning Crs *PRES* * PR1 ... 19 F1
Browning Rd *PRES* PR1 ... 19 F1
Brown La *BER* PR5 ... 25 H4
Brownley St *CHLYE* PR6 ... 37 F3
　CHLYE PR6 ... 45 E3
Browns Hey *CHLY/EC* PR7 ... 40 A5
Brown St *BER* PR5 ... 32 D1
　CHLYE PR6 ... 44 D2
Browsholme Av *FUL/RIB* PR2 ... 13 H5
Brunswick Pl *FUL/RIB* PR2 ... 17 G2
Brunswick St *CHLY/EC* PR7 ... 44 D2
Brydeck Av *PRES* PR1 ... 24 A2
Buchanan St *CHLYE* PR6 ... 44 D3
Buckingham Av *PRES* PR1 ... 23 H4
Buckingham St *CHLYE* PR6 ... 44 D3
Bucklands Av *FUL/RIB* PR2 ... 17 H1
Buckshaw Hall Cl *CHLY/EC* PR7 ... 40 B5
Buckton Cl *CHLYE* PR6 ... 40 C1
Bude Cl *KIRK/FR/WA* PR4 ... 10 D2
Buller Av *PRES* PR1 ... 24 A2
Bulfinch St *PRES* * PR1 ... 18 D2
Bulmer St *FUL/RIB* PR2 ... 17 G1
Burgh Hall Rd *CHLY/EC* PR7 ... 47 E2
Burgh La *CHLY/EC* PR7 ... 47 F3
Burgh La South *CHLY/EC* PR7 ... 47 F3
Burghley Cl *CHLYE* PR6 ... 37 G3
Burghley St *LEYL* * PR25 ... 35 H3
Burgh Mdw *CHLY/EC* PR7 ... 47 G1
Burholme Cl *FUL/RIB* PR2 ... 20 A1
Burholme Pl *FUL/RIB* PR2 ... 20 A1
Burholme Rd *FUL/RIB* PR2 ... 20 A1
Burleigh Rd *PRES* PR1 ... 2 B5
Burlington St *CHLY/EC* PR7 ... 44 D3
Burnsall Pl *FUL/RIB* PR2 ... 13 G4
Burnside Av *FUL/RIB* PR2 ... 13 H5
Burnside Wy *PRES* PR1 ... 23 H3
Burnslack Rd *FUL/RIB* PR2 ... 13 H5
Burns St *PRES* PR1 ... 19 F1
Burrington Cl *FUL/RIB* PR2 ... 13 F2
Burrow Rd *PRES* PR1 ... 3 H1
Burwell Av *CHLY/EC* PR7 ... 46 B5
Burwood Cl *PRES* PR1 ... 24 B4
Burwood Dr *FUL/RIB* PR2 ... 19 G1
Bushell Pl *PRES* PR1 ... 3 G6
Bushell St *PRES* PR1 ... 2 E1
Bussel Rd *PRES* PR1 ... 24 A4
Butcher Brow *BER* PR5 ... 25 G1
Butler Pl *PRES* PR1 ... 18 B1
Butler St *PRES* PR1 ... 2 E5
Butterlands *PRES* PR1 ... 19 H3
Buttermere Av *CHLY/EC* PR7 ... 44 A4
Buttermere Cl *BER* PR5 ... 25 F4
　FUL/RIB PR2 ... 13 E4
Buttermere Rd *GAR/LONG* PR3 ... 15 A5

Butterworth Brow
　CHLY/EC PR7 ... 4
Bymbrig Cl *BER* PR5 ... 3
Byron Crs *CHLY/EC* PR7 ... 4
Byron St *CHLY/EC* PR7 ... 4

C

Cadley Av *FUL/RIB* PR2 ... 1
Cadley Cswy *FUL/RIB* PR2 ... 1
Cadley Dr *FUL/RIB* PR2 ... 1
Cadogan Pl *PRES* PR1 ...
Cage La *KIRK/FR/WA* PR4 ... 3
Cairndale Dr *LEYL* PR25 ...
Cairnsmore Av *PRES* PR1 ... 1
Calder Av *CHLY/EC* PR7 ...
　FUL/RIB PR2 ... 1
　GAR/LONG PR3 ...
Calder St *FUL/RIB* PR2 ... 1
Calfcote La *GAR/LONG* PR3 ... 1
Callon St *PRES* PR1 ... 1
Cambridge Cl *PRES* PR1 ...
Cambridge Rd *BER* PR5 ...
Cambridge St *CHLY/EC* PR7 ... 4
　PRES PR1 ...
Cambridge Wk *PRES* * PR1 ...
Cam Cl *BER* PR5 ...
Camden Pl *PRES* PR1 ...
Camellia Dr *LEYL* PR25 ... 3
Cameron Cft *CHLYE* * PR6 ...
Cam La *BER* PR5 ...
Camomile Cl *CHLY/EC* * PR7 ... 4
Campbell St *PRES* PR1 ...
Campion Dr *FUL/RIB* PR2 ... 1
The Campions *FUL/RIB* PR2 ... 1
Cam St *PRES* PR1 ...
Camwood *BER* PR5 ... 3
Camwood Dr *BER* PR5 ... 2
Cam Wood Fold *CHLYE* PR6 ... 3
Canal Wk *CHLYE* PR6 ...
Canberra Rd *LEYL* PR25 ... 3
Cann Bridge St *BER* PR5 ...
Cannon Hl *FUL/RIB* * PR2 ... 1
Cannon St *PRES* PR1 ...
Canterbury St *CHLYE* PR6 ...
Cantsfield Av *FUL/RIB* PR2 ... 1
Canute St *PRES* PR1 ...
Capesthorne Dr *CHLY/EC* PR7 ... 4
Capitol Wy *PRES* PR1 ...
Cardale *KIRK/FR/WA* PR4 ...
Cardigan La *FUL/RIB* PR2 ...
Carleton Av *FUL/RIB* PR2 ...
Carleton Dr *PRES* PR1 ...
Carleton Rd *CHLYE* PR6 ...
Carlisle Av *PRES* PR1 ...
Carlisle St *PRES* PR1 ...
Carloway Av *FUL/RIB* PR2 ... 1
Carlton Av *CHLYE* PR6 ... 3
Carlton Dr *PRES* PR1 ...
Carlton Rd *LEYL* PR25 ... 3
Carlton St *FUL/RIB* PR2 ...
Carnarvon Rd *PRES* PR1 ...
Carnfield Pl *FUL/RIB* PR2 ... 1
Carnoostie Dr *CHLYE* PR6 ...
Carnoustie Cl *CHLY/EC* PR7 ... 1
Carnoustie Ct *PRES* PR1 ... 1
Caroline St *PRES* PR1 ... 1
Carr Fld *BER* PR5 ... 3
Carr Barn Brow *BER* PR5 ...
Carrington Rd *CHLY/EC* PR7 ... 4
Carr La *CHLY/EC* PR7 ... 4
　LEYL PR25 ... 3
Carr Meadow *BER* PR5 ... 3
Carrol St *PRES* PR1 ...
Carr Pl *BER* PR5 ... 3
Carr Rd *CHLYE* PR6 ...
Carr St *BER* PR5 ... 3
　CHLYE PR6 ... 4
　PRES PR1 ...
Carrwood Rd *BER* PR5 ... 2
Carrwood Wy *BER* PR5 ... 2
Cartmel Dr *BER* PR5 ...
Cartmel Pl *FUL/RIB* PR2 ... 1
Cartmel Rd *LEYL* PR25 ...
Carwood La *CHLYE* PR6 ... 3
Casterton *CHLY/EC* PR7 ...
Castle Fold *PRES* PR1 ...
Castle Mt *FUL/RIB* PR2 ... 1
Castle St *CHLY/EC* PR7 ...
　PRES PR1 ...
Castleton Rd *PRES* PR1 ... 1
Castle Wk *PRES* PR1 ... 1
Catforth Rd *FUL/RIB* PR2 ... 1
Catherine St *CHLY/EC* * PR7 ... 4
　PRES PR1 ...
Cathrow Dr *KIRK/FR/WA* PR4 ... 4

The Crossing *BER* PR5 ....27 H4
Cross Keys Dr *CHLYE* PR6 ....37 G5
Cross St *CHLYE/EC* * PR7 ....44 C1
    GAR/LONG PR3 ....15 A4
    LEYL PR25 ....35 H2
    PRES PR1 ....3 F5
Croston Rd *CROS/BRETH* PR26 .....31 F3
    CROS/BRETH PR26 ....35 E1
Crowell Wy *BER* PR5 ....25 G3
Crow Hills Rd *PRES* PR1 ....17 E5
Crowle St *PRES* PR1 ....19 F3
Crown La *KIRK/FR/WA* PR4 ....4 C3
Crownlee *PRES* PR1 ....23 E3
Crown St *CHLYE/EC* PR7 ....44 C2
    LEYL PR25 ....35 H1
    PRES PR1 ....3 F2
Crummock Rd *PRES* PR1 ....20 A2
Crumpax Av *GAR/LONG* PR3 ....15 B2
Cuerdale La *BER* PR5 ....25 H1
Cuerden Av *LEYL* PR25 ....34 D5
Cuerden Cl *BER* PR5 ....32 C5
Cuerden Ri *BER* PR5 ....32 A2
Cuerden St *CHLYE* PR6 ....32 B1
Cuerden Wy *BER* PR5 ....32 B1
Culbeck La *CHLY/EC* PR7 ....38 B4
Cumberland Av *LEYL* PR25 ....35 E5
Cunliffe St *CHLY/EC* PR7 ....44 C3
    PRES PR1 ....3 H2
Cunnery Meadow *LEYL* PR25 ....36 C3
Cunningham Av *CHLY/EC* PR7 ....44 A4
Curate St *CHLYE* PR6 ....45 E1
Curlew Cl *LEYL* PR25 ....34 C5
Curwen St *PRES* PR1 ....19 E2
Customs Wy *FUL/RIB* PR2 ....17 G3
Cypress Cl *FUL/RIB* PR2 ....14 A4
    LEYL PR25 ....36 C2
Cypress Gv *BER* PR5 ....31 H1

D

Daisy Bank Cl *LEYL* PR25 ....34 D3
Daisy Cft *FUL/RIB* PR2 ....16 B3
Daisyfields *KIRK/FR/WA* * PR4 ......10 D1
Daisy Fold *CHLYE* PR6 ....41 E5
Daisy La *PRES* PR1 ....13 E5
Daisy Meadow *BER* PR5 ....33 F4
Dalby Cl *PRES* PR1 ....13 F5
Dale Av *CHLY/EC* PR7 ....43 B1
    KIRK/FR/WA PR4 ....28 A3
Dalehead Rd *LEYL* PR25 ....38 D1
Dale St *PRES* PR1 ....3 J3
Dale Vw *CHLY/EC* PR7 ....47 D5
Dallas St *PRES* PR1 ....12 A5
Dalmore Rd *FUL/RIB* PR2 ....11 H5
Danes Dr *BER* PR5 ....25 F5
Danesway *BER* PR5 ....25 F5
    PRES PR1 ....23 E2
Danewerke St *PRES* * PR1 ....3 H2
Dark La *CHLYE* PR6 ....41 E1
Dark Wood La *BER* PR5 ....21 H5
Darlington St *CHLY/EC* PR7 ....46 B4
Dart St *FUL/RIB* PR2 ....17 G3
Darwen Cl *GAR/LONG* PR3 ....15 C3
Darwen St *PRES* * PR1 ....19 E4
Darwen Vw *BER* PR5 ....25 G1
Daub Hall La *BER* PR5 ....27 E4
Davis St *GAR/LONG* PR3 ....15 B2
Dawber's La *CHLY/EC* PR7 ....38 A5
Dawnay Rd *FUL/RIB* PR2 ....13 G5
Dawson La *CHLYE* PR6 ....36 C5
Dawson Rd *BER* PR5 ....33 E2
Dawson Wk *PRES* PR1 ....3 F1
Dean St *BER* PR5 ....25 G5
Deborah Av *FUL/RIB* PR2 ....12 C1
Deepdale Houses *PRES* * PR1 ....3 J1
Deepdale Mill St *PRES* PR1 ....3 K1
Deepdale Pk *PRES* * PR1 ....13 F5
Deepdale Rd *PRES* PR1 ....12 D5
    PRES PR1 ....18 D1
Deepdale St *PRES* PR1 ....3 J2
Deerfold *CHLY/EC* PR7 ....40 B5
Deighton Av *LEYL* PR25 ....35 G4
Deighton Rd *CHLY/EC* PR7 ....44 B4
De Lacy St *FUL/RIB* PR2 ....17 H1
Delamere Pl *CHLYE* PR6 ....44 D2
Delaware St *PRES* PR1 ....19 E2
The Dell *CHLYE* PR6 ....41 C4
    FUL/RIB PR2 ....11 H1
The Dellway *KIRK/FR/WA* PR4 ....22 B3
Delph La *CHLY/EC* PR7 ....43 B4
Delph Wy *CHLYE* PR6 ....37 G5
Demming Cl *FUL/RIB* PR2 ....16 A3
Denbigh Cl *LEYL* PR25 ....35 H3
Denbigh Wy *PRES* PR1 ....3 H5

Denby Cl *BER* PR5 ....25 E3
Denford Av *LEYL* PR25 ....35 H4
Denville Rd *PRES* PR1 ....19 E2
Derby Rd *FUL/RIB* PR2 ....12 A4
    GAR/LONG PR3 ....15 B3
Derby Sq *PRES* PR1 ....19 E3
Derby St *LEYL* PR25 ....35 H2
    PRES PR1 ....3 H3
Derek Rd *CHLYE* PR6 ....37 G3
Derry Rd *FUL/RIB* PR2 ....13 G5
Derwent Dr *BER* PR5 ....15 A5
Derwent Rd *CHLY/EC* PR7 ....44 B5
Derwentwater Pl *PRES* * PR1 ....18 B1
Dever Av *PRES* PR1 ....34 D3
Devon Cl *BER* PR5 ....25 F3
Devonport Cl *BER* PR5 ....25 G3
Devonport Wy *CHLYE* PR6 ....45 E2
Devonshire Ct *CHLY/EC* PR7 ....44 C2
Devonshire Pl *PRES* PR1 ....19 C2
Devonshire Rd *CHLY/EC* PR7 ....44 C3
    FUL/RIB PR2 ....12 C4
Dewhurst Rw *BER* PR5 ....32 B3
Dewhurst St *PRES* PR1 ....2 B1
Dickens Rd *CHLY/EC* PR7 ....46 C5
Dickson Av *PRES* PR1 ....19 F1
Dickson Hey *KIRK/FR/WA* PR4 ......29 D1
Dickson St *PRES* * PR1 ....3 J5
Dilworth Ct *GAR/LONG* PR3 ....15 C4
Dilworth La *GAR/LONG* PR3 ....15 C3
The Dingle *CHLYE* PR6 ....41 G4
    FUL/RIB PR2 ....11 H1
Dixon Rd *GAR/LONG* PR3 ....15 C3
Dixons La *FUL/RIB* PR2 ....9 G3
Dob Brow *CHLY/EC* PR7 ....46 D1
Doctor's La *CHLY/EC* PR7 ....42 A4
Doctors Rw *GAR/LONG* PR3 ....15 B4
Dodd Wy *BER* PR5 ....33 E3
Dodgson Pl *PRES* PR1 ....19 E2
Dodgson Rd *PRES* PR1 ....19 E2
Dodney Dr *FUL/RIB* PR2 ....16 A2
Dole La *CHLY/EC* PR7 ....44 C2
Doodstone Av *BER* PR5 ....24 D5
Doodstone Cl *BER* PR5 ....24 D5
Doodstone Nook *BER* PR5 ....24 D5
Doris St *CHLYE* PR6 ....44 D1
Dorking Rd *CHLYE* PR6 ....41 F3
Dorman Rd *FUL/RIB* PR2 ....13 G5
Dorothy Av *LEYL* PR25 ....35 G3
Dorset Rd *PRES* PR1 ....18 C2
Douglas Av *BER* * PR5 ....32 D1
Douglas Ct *FUL/RIB* PR2 ....11 H5
Douglas Rd *FUL/RIB* PR2 ....11 H5
Douglas Rd North *FUL/RIB* PR2 .....11 H5
Douglas St *FUL/RIB* PR2 ....17 G2
The Doultons *BER* PR5 ....25 E3
Dove Av *PRES* PR1 ....24 A2
Dovecote *CHLYE* PR6 ....37 E1
Dovedale Av *FUL/RIB* PR2 ....11 E4
Dovedale Cl *FUL/RIB* PR2 ....11 E4
    LEYL PR25 ....38 C1
Dove St *PRES* PR1 ....18 D2
Dovetree Cl *BER* * PR5 ....24 D3
Downham Rd *LEYL* PR25 ....34 C4
Downing Ct *GAR/LONG* PR3 ....6 C2
Downing St *PRES* PR1 ....19 G3
Drakes Cft *FUL/RIB* PR2 ....11 G5
Drakes Hollow *BER* PR5 ....25 F2
Drapers Av *CHLY/EC* PR7 ....42 C4
Driscoll St *PRES* PR1 ....3 J2
The Drive *BER* PR5 ....25 H1
    FUL/RIB PR2 ....12 C4
    KIRK/FR/WA PR4 ....28 C2
Drumacre La East
    KIRK/FR/WA PR4 ....29 A3
Drumacre La West
    KIRK/FR/WA PR4 ....28 C4
Drumhead Rd *CHLYE* PR6 ....40 D5
Duchy Av *FUL/RIB* PR2 ....12 D4
Ducie Pl *PRES* PR1 ....19 H2
Duddle La *BER* PR5 ....25 F4
Dudley Cl *KIRK/FR/WA* PR4 ....28 C1
Dukes Meadow *FUL/RIB* PR2 ....11 E3
Duke St *BER* PR5 ....32 C2
    CHLY/EC PR7 ....44 C4
    PRES PR1 ....3 J4
Dunbar Dr *FUL/RIB* PR2 ....11 H4
Dunbar Rd *FUL/RIB* PR2 ....10 D5
Dunderdale St *GAR/LONG* PR3 ....15 C5
Dundonald St *PRES* PR1 ....19 F3
Dunham Dr *CHLYE* PR6 ....40 C2
Dunkirk Av *FUL/RIB* PR2 ....11 G4
Dunkirk La *CROS/BRETH* PR26 ....34 A3
    LEYL PR25 ....34 D4
Dunmore St *PRES* PR1 ....3 K2
Dunnock La *KIRK/FR/WA* PR4 ....10 C4
Dunoon Cl *FUL/RIB* PR2 ....10 D4
Dunrobin Dr *CHLY/EC* PR7 ....43 B1
Dunscar Dr *CHLYE* PR6 ....45 E1

Dunsop Cl *BER* * PR5 ....32 D1
Dunsop Rd *FUL/RIB* PR2 ....13 F4
D'Urton La *GAR/LONG* PR3 ....7 E4
Dutch Barn Cl *CHLY/EC* PR7 ....40 B4
Duttonfield Cl
    CROS/BRETH PR26 ....35 E1
Duxbury Hall Rd *CHLY/EC* PR7 ......47 H1
Dymock Rd *PRES* * PR1 ....19 F2
Dymock Rd North *PRES* * PR1 ....19 F2

E

Ealing Gv *CHLYE* PR6 ....41 F5
Earls Av *BER* PR5 ....32 C1
Earl St *PRES* PR1 ....3 F5
Earls Wy *CHLY/EC* PR7 ....39 F5
Earnshaw Dr *LEYL* PR25 ....34 D3
Eastbourne Cl *FUL/RIB* PR2 ....10 D3
East Cliff *PRES* PR1 ....2 E6
East Cliff Rd *PRES* PR1 ....2 E6
Eastfield Dr *KIRK/FR/WA* PR4 ....28 C1
Eastgate *FUL/RIB* PR2 ....11 H3
Eastham St *PRES* PR1 ....18 A2
Eastlands *CROS/BRETH* PR26 ....34 C5
Easton Cl *FUL/RIB* PR2 ....13 F2
East Rd *FUL/RIB* PR2 ....12 C4
East Sq *KIRK/FR/WA* PR4 ....28 C1
East St *BER* PR5 ....32 C2
    LEYL PR25 ....35 H1
    LEYL PR25 ....35 H3
    PRES PR1 ....3 H1
East Ter *CHLYE* PR6 ....39 G3
East Vw *BER* PR5 ....19 E5
    PRES PR1 ....3 H1
East Wy *CHLYE* PR6 ....44 D2
Eastway *FUL/RIB* PR2 ....7 G5
    FUL/RIB PR2 ....12 D2
    GAR/LONG PR3 ....6 C5
Eastwood Rd *LEYL* PR25 ....35 F3
Eaves Green Rd *CHLY/EC* PR7 ....44 B5
Eaves La *CHLYE* PR6 ....45 E3
    FUL/RIB PR2 ....12 A5
Eaveswood Cl *BER* PR5 ....25 C5
Eccles St *PRES* PR1 ....19 E2
Ecroyd Rd *FUL/RIB* * PR2 ....17 G1
Ecroyd St *LEYL* PR25 ....35 G3
Edale Cl *LEYL* PR25 ....35 G5
Edale Ct *PRES* PR1 ....18 B2
Eden Gdns *GAR/LONG* PR3 ....15 C2
Eden St *LEYL* PR25 ....35 G4
Edenway *FUL/RIB* PR2 ....11 H1
Edgefield *CHLY/EC* PR7 ....40 B5
Edgehill Cl *FUL/RIB* PR2 ....11 H4
Edgehill Crs *LEYL* PR25 ....35 E2
Edgehill Dr *FUL/RIB* PR2 ....11 H4
Edinburgh Cl *LEYL* PR25 ....36 A3
Edmund St *PRES* PR1 ....3 J3
Edward Sq *PRES* PR1 ....3 H1
Edward St *BER* PR5 ....25 E1
    BER PR5 ....32 C1
    CHLYE PR6 ....44 D3
    LEYL PR25 ....35 G4
    PRES PR1 ....2 E3
Edward VII Quay *FUL/RIB* * PR2 .....17 F3
Egan St *PRES* PR1 ....3 H2
Egbert St *PRES* PR1 ....18 C2
Egerton Ct *FUL/RIB* * PR2 ....17 F2
Egerton Gv *CHLY/EC* PR7 ....44 B4
Egerton Rd *CHLY/EC* PR7 ....17 F2
    LEYL PR25 ....35 F2
Elcho St *CHLY/EC* PR7 ....44 C3
Elcho St *PRES* PR1 ....18 C1
Elder Cl *CHLYE* PR6 ....37 G2
    FUL/RIB PR2 ....13 F2
Eldon St *CHLYE* PR6 ....44 D3
    PRES PR1 ....18 A1
Elgin St *PRES* PR1 ....18 C1
Elijah St *PRES* PR1 ....19 F3
Elizabeth Sq *PRES* PR1 ....3 H1
Elizabeth St *PRES* PR1 ....3 F2
Ellen Ct *PRES* PR1 ....18 B1
Ellen St *BER* PR5 ....25 G5
    PRES PR1 ....17 H2
Ellerbeck Av *FUL/RIB* PR2 ....13 G3
Ellerslie Rd *FUL/RIB* PR2 ....17 F2
Elliott Cl *PRES* PR1 ....18 A1
Elliott St *PRES* PR1 ....18 A2
Elliott Wk *PRES* PR1 ....18 A2
Elm Av *FUL/RIB* PR2 ....16 D1
Elm Dr *BER* PR5 ....25 H5
Elmfield Dr *BER* PR5 ....33 G4
Elm Gv *CHLYE* PR6 ....41 E5
    FUL/RIB PR2 ....19 G1
    LEYL PR25 ....36 B1
The Elms *CHLYE* PR6 ....37 G2
Elmsley St *PRES* PR1 ....12 A5

Elmwood *CHLY/EC* PR7 ....4[?]
    GAR/LONG PR3 ....4[?]
Elmwood Av *LEYL* PR25 ....35[?]
Elmwood Dr *PRES* PR1 ....4[?]
Elswick Rd *FUL/RIB* PR2 ....17[?]
    LEYL PR25 ....35[?]
Elton St *FUL/RIB* PR2 ....4[?]
Emerson Rd *PRES* PR1 ....4[?]
Emily St *BER* PR5 ....2[?]
Emlsett Rd *BER* PR5 ....4[?]
Emmanuel St *FUL/RIB* PR2 ....4[?]
Emmett St *PRES* PR1 ....4[?]
Empress Av *FUL/RIB* PR2 ....4[?]
Empress Wy *CHLY/EC* PR7 ....2[?]
Endeavour Cl *FUL/RIB* PR2 ....4[?]
Enfield Cl *CHLY/EC* PR7 ....4[?]
English Martyrs' Pl *PRES* PR1 ....4[?]
Ennerdale Cl *LEYL* PR25 ....3[?]
Ennerdale Dr *BER* PR5 ....2[?]
Ennerdale Rd *CHLY/EC* PR7 ....4[?]
    GAR/LONG PR3 ....3[?]
Ephraim St *PRES* PR1 ....4[?]
Epping Pl *CHLYE* PR6 ....4[?]
Epsom Cl *CHLYE* PR6 ....4[?]
Erskine Rd *CHLYE* PR6 ....4[?]
Esher Pond *FUL/RIB* PR2 ....1[?]
Eskdale Cl *FUL/RIB* PR2 ....1[?]
Eskdale Rd *GAR/LONG* PR3 ....1[?]
    LEYL PR25 ....3[?]
The Esplanade *PRES* PR1 ....2[?]
Esplanade *PRES* PR1 ....2[?]
Essex St *PRES* PR1 ....1[?]
Eton Pk *FUL/RIB* PR2 ....1[?]
Euston St *PRES* PR1 ....1[?]
Euxton Hall Gdns *CHLY/EC* PR7 .....3[?]
Euxton La *CHLY/EC* PR7 ....3[?]
    CHLY/EC PR7 ....3[?]
Evans St *FUL/RIB* PR2 ....1[?]
Evergreen Av *LEYL* PR25 ....3[?]
Evergreen Cl *CHLY/EC* PR7 ....4[?]
The Evergreens
    KIRK/FR/WA PR4 ....1[?]
Eversleigh St *PRES* PR1 ....1[?]
Evesham Av *PRES* PR1 ....1[?]
Evesham Cl *KIRK/FR/WA* PR4 ....4[?]
Ewell Cl *CHLYE* PR6 ....1[?]
Exe St *PRES* PR1 ....1[?]
Exeter Pl *FUL/RIB* PR2 ....1[?]

F

Factory La *PRES* PR1 ....2[?]
Fairfax Pl *BER* PR5 ....3[?]
Fairfax Rd *FUL/RIB* PR2 ....1[?]
Fairfield Dr *FUL/RIB* * PR2 ....1[?]
Fairfield Rd *FUL/RIB* PR2 ....1[?]
    LEYL PR25 ....3[?]
Fairfield St *BER* PR5 ....3[?]
Fairham Av *PRES* * PR1 ....3[?]
Fairhaven Rd *LEYL* PR25 ....3[?]
    PRES PR1 ....2[?]
Fair Oak Cl *FUL/RIB* PR2 ....2[?]
Fairsnape Av *GAR/LONG* PR3 ....1[?]
Fairview Cl *KIRK/FR/WA* PR4 ....2[?]
Fairway *CHLY/EC* PR7 ....4[?]
    PRES PR1 ....1[?]
Fairways Av *GAR/LONG* PR3 ....[?]
Falcon St *PRES* PR1 ....1[?]
Falkland St *PRES* PR1 ....2[?]
Faraday Dr *FUL/RIB* PR2 ....1[?]
Far Cft *BER* PR5 ....2[?]
Fareham Cl *BER* PR5 ....2[?]
Far Fld *FUL/RIB* PR2 ....2[?]
Farington Av *LEYL* PR25 ....3[?]
Farington Ga *LEYL* PR25 ....3[?]
Farington Rd
    CROS/BRETH PR26 ....3[?]
Far La *PRES* PR1 ....2[?]
Farmend Cl *KIRK/FR/WA* PR4 ....2[?]
Farm House Cl *CHLYE* PR6 ....4[?]
Far Nook *CHLYE* PR6 ....4[?]
Farringdon Cl *PRES* PR1 ....1[?]
Farringdon Crs *FUL/RIB* PR2 ....1[?]
Farringdon La *FUL/RIB* PR2 ....1[?]
Farringdon Pl *FUL/RIB* PR2 ....1[?]
Farrington St *CHLY/EC* PR7 ....4[?]
The Farthings *CHLY/EC* PR7 ....4[?]
Fazackerley St *FUL/RIB* PR2 ....1[?]
Fazackerley St *CHLY/EC* PR7 ....1[?]
Fell Brow *GAR/LONG* PR3 ....1[?]
Fell Cl *BER* PR5 ....3[?]
Fellery St *CHLY/EC* PR7 ....4[?]
Fell Vw *CHLYE* PR6 ....3[?]
    FUL/RIB PR2 ....3[?]
Fellway Cl *BER* PR5 ....3[?]

ad St PRES PR1 ......19 F3
ove KIRK/FR/WA PR4 ......28 C2
vy KIRK/FR/WA PR4 ......22 B4
n Rd FUL/RIB PR2 ......13 E4
r Rd PRES PR1 ......19 G2
Bank CHLYE PR6 ......40 D4
CI BER PR5 ......31 H1
ale CI LEYL PR25 ......35 H5
eigh CROS/BRETH PR26 ......34 A4
Meadow CHLYE PR6 ......37 G2
erns BER PR5 ......45 E3
/RIB PR2 ......17 G1
halgh Ct FUL/RIB * PR2 ......13 F2
halgh Gdns FUL/RIB PR2 ......13 F2
halgh La FUL/RIB PR2 ......8 A5
halgh PI FUL/RIB PR2 ......13 F2
r's La CHLYE PR6 ......37 F2
La CROS/BRETH PR26 ......31 F3
n St CHLYE PR6 ......45 E2
L PR25 ......34 D3
Maple Dr FUL/RIB PR2 ......13 H4
ields CHLY/EC PR7 ......43 A2
side Av CHLY/EC PR7 ......43 A2
side CI BER PR5 ......45 E4
I CHLYE PR6 ......45 E4
ilberts FUL/RIB PR2 ......11 G4
ts CI CHLY/EC PR7 ......44 C3
PI FUL/RIB PR2 ......11 E4
es Cottages PRES * PR1 ......24 A2
La KIRK/FR/WA PR4 ......10 C4
y Park Dr FUL/RIB PR2 ......16 B3
nk CHLY/EC PR7 ......39 E5
Av FUL/RIB PR2 ......17 E1
ee Av FUL/RIB PR2 ......11 H4
e CI CHLY/EC PR7 ......47 G2
ees Av FUL/RIB PR2 ......13 H4
K/FR/WA PR4 ......24 B5
ees Crs BER PR5 ......13 H4
ees PI FUL/RIB PR2 ......13 H4
ees Rd BER PR5 ......24 C5
od La BER PR5 ......27 H1
rgate PRES PR1 ......2 D5
rgate Ct PRES * PR1 ......2 D5
rgate HI PRES PR1 ......2 C6
t PRES PR1 ......3 F1
vick Pde PRES PR1 ......19 F3
vick Rd PRES PR1 ......19 F3
vick Vw PRES PR1 ......19 F3
field PRES PR1 ......28 B4
erald St PRES PR1 ......19 E2
by St PRES PR1 ......2 B4
Acres CROS/BRETH PR26 ......31 E5
La CHLYE PR6 ......45 F5
ES PR1 ......2 E4
St CHLY/EC PR7 ......44 C3
R/LONG PR3 ......15 B3
ES PR1 ......2 E4
wood St FUL/RIB PR2 ......2 A1
L PR25 ......35 H2
burg Wy
DS/BRETH PR26 ......34 D1
Rd PRES PR1 ......3 J2
St FUL/RIB PR2 ......17 G2
off Wy PRES PR1 ......12 D5
erfield KIRK/FR/WA PR4 ......10 C2
I Rd FUL/RIB * PR2 ......13 G5
r St PRES PR1 ......3 K4
gate FUL/RIB PR2 ......12 B4
st CI BER PR5 ......25 E3
st Wy FUL/RIB PR2 ......12 B3
stway LEYL PR25 ......35 F4
by Crs KIRK/FR/WA PR4 ......28 B3
by PI FUL/RIB PR2 ......16 C1
ester CI LEYL PR25 ......35 E3
aw Rd PRES PR1 ......23 H4
n Rd FUL/RIB PR2 ......16 C3
Acre La GAR/LONG PR3 ......15 D1
dale Moss
DS/BRETH PR26 ......34 C3
Cft PRES PR1 ......17 G5
erfield PI CHLYE PR6 ......45 E1
r St CHLYE PR6 ......45 E1
dry St CHLY/EC * PR7 ......44 C2
tains CI CHLY/EC PR7 ......44 D5
ields BER PR5 ......25 G5
Lane Ends BER PR5 ......26 D4
Oaks Rd BER PR5 ......33 E3
er Av CROS/BRETH PR26 ......31 H3
er CI BER PR5 ......27 H4
er La CROS/BRETH PR26 ......31 G3
er St FUL/RIB PR2 ......11 H5
ote CHLY/EC PR7 ......40 B5
ale Gv PRES PR1 ......13 F5
love Dr CHLYE PR6 ......40 B2
ole Rd CHLY/EC PR7 ......43 C1
a BER PR5 ......27 E3

LEYL PR25 ......34 D4
Fox St PRES PR1 ......2 E4
The Foxwood CHLY/EC PR7 ......46 A4
Francis St FUL/RIB PR2 ......17 G2
Franklands CI KIRK/FR/WA PR4 ......28 C1
Franklands Dr FUL/RIB PR2 ......13 H3
Franklands Fold
    KIRK/FR/WA PR4 ......28 C2
Frank St PRES PR1 ......18 B2
Fraser Av PRES PR1 ......24 A2
Frederick St PRES PR1 ......45 E3
Frenchwood Av PRES PR1 ......3 K6
Frenchwood Knoll PRES PR1 ......3 J7
Frenchwood St PRES PR1 ......3 H6
Freshfields FUL/RIB PR2 ......10 B5
Friargate PRES PR1 ......2 E2
The Friars FUL/RIB PR2 ......2 A4
Friday St CHLYE PR6 ......44 D2
Friths Av BER PR5 ......27 E5
Frome St PRES PR1 ......19 F2
Froom St CHLYE PR6 ......45 E2
Fryers CI PRES PR1 ......23 G5
Fulford Av FUL/RIB PR2 ......17 F1
Fulshaw Rd FUL/RIB PR2 ......17 F1
Fulwood Hall La FUL/RIB PR2 ......12 D4
Fulwood Hts FUL/RIB PR2 ......13 E3
Fulwood Rw FUL/RIB PR2 ......13 E3
Furness CI CHLY/EC PR7 ......44 D5
Further Fld BER PR5 ......33 E1
Fylde Rd PRES PR1 ......2 C1
Fylde St PRES PR1 ......2 D2

G

The Gables KIRK/FR/WA PR4 ......10 C4
Gainsborough Av BER PR5 ......31 G2
Gamull La FUL/RIB PR2 ......13 H3
Ganton Ct PRES PR1 ......17 E5
Garden St PRES PR1 ......2 E5
Garden Ter CHLY/EC PR7 ......44 C1
Garden Wk FUL/RIB PR2 ......17 F2
Gardner St PRES PR1 ......3 F2
Garfield Ter CHLYE PR6 ......40 D5
Garrison Rd FUL/RIB PR2 ......12 D5
Garsdale CI BER PR5 ......25 G5
Garsdale Rd FUL/RIB PR2 ......13 G4
Garstang Rd FUL/RIB PR2 ......12 A3
    FUL/RIB PR2 ......12 A3
Garstone Cft FUL/RIB PR2 ......17 H5
Gaskell Rd PRES PR1 ......24 A1
Gaskell St CHLYE PR6 ......35 E2
Gas Ter LEYL PR25 ......35 H2
Gatesgarth Av FUL/RIB PR2 ......12 B1
Gathurst Rd FUL/RIB PR2 ......17 G1
Gaythorne Av PRES PR1 ......19 H2
Geneva Rd FUL/RIB PR2 ......13 E4
Geoffrey St CHLYE PR6 ......44 D1
    PRES PR1 ......19 E2
George's Rd PRES PR1 ......3 H4
George St CHLY/EC PR7 ......44 C3
    GAR/LONG PR3 ......15 G1
    LEYL PR25 ......35 H2
    PRES PR1 ......3 K4
German La CHLY/EC PR7 ......43 B2
Gerrard St PRES PR1 ......2 B4
Gilbert St CHLY/EC * PR7 ......44 C4
Gildow St PRES PR1 ......2 C3
Gilhouse Av FUL/RIB PR2 ......16 A2
Gillcroft CHLY/EC PR7 ......42 B3
Giller CI PRES PR1 ......24 A4
Giller Dr PRES PR1 ......24 A4
Giller Fold PRES PR1 ......24 B4
Gillett St PRES PR1 ......19 E2
Gillibrand CI PRES PR1 ......23 D3
Gillibrand St BER PR5 ......25 F1
    CHLY/EC PR7 ......44 C4
Gillibrand Wks CHLY/EC PR7 ......44 C4
Gill La KIRK/FR/WA PR4 ......28 C5
Gill Nook KIRK/FR/WA PR4 ......28 C5
Gin Bow CHLY/EC PR7 ......44 C4
Gisburn Rd FUL/RIB PR2 ......13 G4
Glamis Dr CHLY/EC PR7 ......44 B2
Glamis Rd LEYL PR25 ......36 A4
The Glebe CROS/BRETH PR26 ......34 B4
Glebe CI FUL/RIB PR2 ......12 B4
The Glen FUL/RIB PR2 ......19 H1
Glencourse Dr FUL/RIB PR2 ......13 E3
Glencroft CHLY/EC PR7 ......38 D4
Glendale Av BER PR5 ......25 E5
Glendale CI FUL/RIB PR2 ......35 H5
Glendale Crs BER PR5 ......25 E5
Glendale Gv FUL/RIB PR2 ......19 F1
Gleneagles Dr CHLYE PR6 ......39 F5
    FUL/RIB PR2 ......11 F1
    PRES PR1 ......17 E5

Glen Gv FUL/RIB PR2 ......13 H3
Glenluce Dr PRES PR1 ......19 H3
Glenmore CHLYE PR6 ......37 E2
Glenview CI FUL/RIB PR2 ......14 A5
Glenview Ct FUL/RIB PR2 ......14 A5
Glenway PRES PR1 ......23 G2
Gloucester Av LEYL PR25 ......36 A1
Gloucester Rd CHLY/EC PR7 ......44 C5
Glover's Ct PRES PR1 ......3 G4
Glover St PRES PR1 ......3 G5
Golbourne St PRES PR1 ......3 J1
Goldburn CI FUL/RIB PR2 ......10 D2
Golden HI LEYL PR25 ......35 H2
Golden Hill La LEYL PR25 ......35 E2
Golden Wy PRES PR1 ......23 H2
Goldfinch St PRES PR1 ......18 D1
Golf Vw FUL/RIB PR2 ......11 E2
Good St PRES PR1 ......2 C5
Goodwood Av FUL/RIB PR2 ......12 B1
Goose Green Av PRES PR1 ......46 D4
Gordon St CHLYE PR6 ......44 D3
    PRES PR1 ......2 C1
Goring St CHLY/EC PR7 ......44 D3
Gorse CI CHLYE PR6 ......41 E5
Gorse Gv FUL/RIB PR2 ......13 C5
    KIRK/FR/WA PR4 ......28 C1
Gorsewood LEYL PR25 ......35 E3
Gough La BER PR5 ......33 F4
Goulding Av LEYL PR25 ......35 H3
Goulding St CHLY/EC PR7 ......44 D4
Gower St CROS/BRETH PR26 ......34 D2
Gradwell St PRES PR1 ......2 C3
Grafton Ct CHLY/EC PR7 ......44 B5
Grafton Rd FUL/RIB PR2 ......13 H4
Grafton St PRES PR1 ......2 C6
Graham Av BER PR5 ......32 A1
Graham St PRES PR1 ......18 D2
The Grange KIRK/FR/WA PR4 ......10 C3
Grange Av FUL/RIB PR2 ......14 A4
    FUL/RIB PR2 ......14 A4
Grange Dr BER PR5 ......26 D2
    CHLY/EC PR7 ......46 B5
    CHLYE PR6 ......39 E3
Grangefield KIRK/FR/WA PR4 ......28 B1
Grange Park CI PRES PR1 ......17 E5
Grange PI FUL/RIB PR2 ......13 H4
Grange Rd FUL/RIB PR2 ......11 G5
    LEYL PR25 ......34 D3
The Granings KIRK/FR/WA PR4 ......10 B2
Grant Dr KIRK/FR/WA PR4 ......28 C5
Granville Rd CHLYE PR6 ......45 E1
Grasmere Av LEYL PR25 ......35 G1
Grasmere CI BER PR5 ......25 F4
    CHLY/EC PR7 ......43 B1
    FUL/RIB PR2 ......13 E4
Grasmere Gv CHLYE PR6 ......37 F5
    GAR/LONG PR3 ......15 A5
Grasmere Ter CHLY/EC PR7 ......44 B5
Great Avenham St PRES PR1 ......3 G6
Great George St PRES PR1 ......3 F1
Great Gill KIRK/FR/WA PR4 ......28 C5
Great Greens La BER PR5 ......33 F4
Great Hanover St PRES PR1 ......18 C2
Great Meadow BER PR5 ......31 G1
    CHLY/EC PR7 ......40 A5
Great Shaw St PRES PR1 ......2 E3
Great Townley St PRES PR1 ......19 F3
Great Tunstead
    KIRK/FR/WA PR4 ......28 C3
Greaves Meadow PRES PR1 ......24 A5
Greaves St PRES * PR1 ......3 H4
Greaves-Town La FUL/RIB PR2 ......16 C2
The Green CHLY/EC PR7 ......42 C5
    FUL/RIB PR2 ......19 H2
The Greenacres
    KIRK/FR/WA PR4 ......22 B4
Greenacres FUL/RIB PR2 ......11 F1
Greenacres Dr CHLYE PR6 ......39 F3
Greenbank Av PRES PR1 ......17 H1
Greenbank PI PRES PR1 ......2 C1
Greenbank Rd PRES PR1 ......24 A2
Greenbank St PRES PR1 ......17 H1
Greencroft PRES PR1 ......23 H3
Greendale Ms FUL/RIB PR2 ......16 C1
Green Dr BER PR5 ......25 F3
    FUL/RIB PR2 ......12 A1
    PRES PR1 ......23 H3
Greenfield Dr BER PR5 ......31 G1
Greenfield Rd CHLYE PR6 ......45 E1
Greenfield Wy FUL/RIB PR2 ......11 F3
Green Ga FUL/RIB PR2 ......11 F3
    KIRK/FR/WA PR4 ......22 A5
Greenlands Crs FUL/RIB PR2 ......11 G5
Green La BER PR5 ......21 F5
    CROS/BRETH PR26 ......31 E2
    GAR/LONG PR3 ......15 C2
    KIRK/FR/WA PR4 ......23 G5
Greenmead CI KIRK/FR/WA PR4 ......10 C3

Green Nook La GAR/LONG PR3 ......15 A4
Green PI BER PR5 ......33 E3
Greenside CHLY/EC PR7 ......39 E4
Greenside Av FUL/RIB PR2 ......16 A2
Greenside Gdns
    CROS/BRETH PR26 ......34 B5
Green St CHLY/EC PR7 ......44 A5
Greensway GAR/LONG PR3 ......6 C2
Greenthorn Crs FUL/RIB PR2 ......20 A1
Greenway CHLY/EC PR7 ......42 B3
    FUL/RIB PR2 ......11 H1
    PRES PR1 ......23 F2
Greenwood BER PR5 ......33 F5
Greenwood St BER PR5 ......25 G5
    PRES PR1 ......3 J4
Gregson La BER PR5 ......26 C4
Gregson Wy FUL/RIB PR2 ......12 D3
Grenville Av BER PR5 ......25 F4
Greyfriars Av FUL/RIB PR2 ......11 H3
Greyfriars Crs FUL/RIB PR2 ......11 H3
Greyfriars Dr PRES PR1 ......23 G1
Grey Heights Vw CHLYE PR6 ......45 E2
Greystock Av FUL/RIB PR2 ......12 A2
Greystock CI BER PR5 ......33 F1
Greystones CROS/BRETH PR26 ......34 B3
Grime St CHLY/EC PR7 ......44 D4
Grimsargh St PRES * PR1 ......19 F2
Grimshaw St PRES PR1 ......3 H4
Grisedale PI CHLY/EC PR7 ......44 B5
Grizedale CI FUL/RIB PR2 ......19 H1
Grizedale Crs FUL/RIB PR2 ......20 A1
Grizedale PI FUL/RIB PR2 ......19 H1
The Grove CHLYE PR6 ......40 C5
    PRES PR1 ......23 F2
Grosvenor PI FUL/RIB PR2 ......17 F1
Grosvenor Rd CHLY/EC PR7 ......44 A4
Grosvenor St PRES PR1 ......3 K4
Grove Av KIRK/FR/WA PR4 ......28 B2
Grove Rd BER PR5 ......19 E5
Grove St BER PR5 ......32 D1
    LEYL PR25 ......34 D4
Grundy's La CHLY/EC PR7 ......47 G4
Grundy St LEYL PR25 ......35 G2
Guildford Av CHLYE PR6 ......41 F3
Guildford Rd PRES PR1 ......3 G5
Guild Hall Ar PRES * PR1 ......3 G4
Guildhall St PRES PR1 ......3 G5
Guild Rw PRES PR1 ......3 G4
Guild Wy BER PR5 ......2 A5

H

Hacking Dr GAR/LONG PR3 ......15 A5
Haddon PI FUL/RIB PR2 ......11 H5
Haig Av FUL/RIB * PR2 ......17 H1
    LEYL PR25 ......35 F3
Haigh CI CHLY/EC PR7 ......44 A3
Haigh Crs FUL/RIB PR2 ......44 A3
Haighton Ct FUL/RIB PR2 ......12 C1
Haighton Dr FUL/RIB PR2 ......13 G2
Haighton Green La FUL/RIB PR2 ......8 C3
Half Acre BER PR5 ......31 G1
Halfpenny La GAR/LONG PR3 ......15 A3
Hall Cft KIRK/FR/WA PR4 ......22 B4
Hall Ga CHLY/EC PR7 ......44 A1
Halliwell La CHLYE PR6 ......40 C3
Halliwell PI CHLY/EC * PR7 ......44 C3
Halliwell St CHLY/EC PR7 ......44 C3
Hall La LEYL PR25 ......35 F2
Hall Rd FUL/RIB PR2 ......12 A3
    PRES PR1 ......24 A3
Halls Sq CHLYE * PR6 ......41 E1
Hall St FUL/RIB PR2 ......17 G2
Hallwood Rd CHLY/EC PR7 ......44 A5
Halsbury St PRES PR1 ......3 J6
Halstead Rd FUL/RIB PR2 ......13 F3
Halton Av LEYL PR25 ......36 B2
Halton PI FUL/RIB PR2 ......13 H4
    GAR/LONG PR3 ......15 C2
Hambledon Dr PRES PR1 ......24 A4
Hambleton CI KIRK/FR/WA PR4 ......28 B1
Hamer Rd FUL/RIB PR2 ......11 H5
Hamilton Gv FUL/RIB PR2 ......13 G4
Hamilton Rd CHLY/EC PR7 ......44 B3
    FUL/RIB PR2 ......13 F5
Hammond Ct PRES PR1 ......18 A2
Hammond's Rw PRES * PR1 ......3 H4
Hammond St PRES * PR1 ......18 A1
    PRES PR1 ......18 A2
    PRES * PR1 ......18 B1
Hampden PI LEYL PR25 ......35 G2
Hampshire Rd BER PR5 ......25 F3
Hampson Av LEYL PR25 ......36 B3
Hampstead Rd FUL/RIB PR2 ......19 F1
Hampton CI CHLY/EC PR7 ......44 B2
Hampton St FUL/RIB PR2 ......17 G1

Hanbury St *FUL/RIB* * PR2 ....17 G2
The Handbridge *FUL/RIB* PR2 ....12 A3
Hanover St *PRES* PR1 ....3 F1
Harcourt St *PRES* PR1 ....18 A2
Hardacre La *CHLYE* PR6 ....40 B2
Hardcastle Rd *FUL/RIB* PR2 ....12 A5
Hardwicke St *PRES* * PR1 ....3 G2
Hardy Dr *CHLY/EC* PR7 ....44 A4
Hareden Cl *BER* PR5 ....32 D1
Hareden Rd *FUL/RIB* PR2 ....19 H1
Harestone Av *CHLY/EC* PR7 ....44 A5
Harewood Rd *PRES* PR1 ....18 D1
Hargreaves Av *LEYL* PR25 ....35 H4
Hargreaves Ct *FUL/RIB* PR2 ....10 D4
Harland St *FUL/RIB* PR2 ....11 H5
Harlech Dr *LEYL* PR25 ....35 H3
Harling Rd *PRES* PR1 ....19 F2
Harold Ter *BER* PR5 ....31 G1
Harperley *CHLY/EC* PR7 ....40 B5
Harper's La *CHLY/EC* PR7 ....44 D1
Harrington Rd *CHLY/EC* PR7 ....44 B2
Harrington St *PRES* PR1 ....2 D2
Harris Knowledge Pk
    FUL/RIB * PR2 ....12 A3
Harrison La *KIRK/FR/WA* PR4 ....23 F4
Harrison Rd *CHLY/EC* PR7 ....44 C4
    FUL/RIB PR2 ....12 A3
Harris St *PRES* PR1 ....3 G4
Harrock Rd *LEYL* PR25 ....36 B3
Harrop Pl *FUL/RIB* PR2 ....2 A4
Hartington Rd *PRES* PR1 ....2 B5
Hartwood Gn *CHLYE* PR6 ....40 C4
Harvest Dr *CHLYE* PR6 ....40 C1
Hassett Cl *PRES* PR1 ....2 C7
Hastings Rd *FUL/RIB* PR2 ....17 F2
    LEYL PR25 ....35 H2
Hatfield Rd *FUL/RIB* PR2 ....13 G5
Havelock Rd *BER* PR5 ....32 C2
    PRES PR1 ....24 A1
Havelock St *PRES* PR1 ....17 H2
Hawarden Rd *PRES* PR1 ....19 G2
Haweswater Av *CHLY/EC* PR7 ....44 B4
Hawkhurst Av *FUL/RIB* PR2 ....11 H2
Hawkhurst Crs *FUL/RIB* PR2 ....11 H1
Hawkhurst Rd *PRES* PR1 ....18 D1
    PRES PR1 ....24 A2
Hawkins Cl *PRES* PR1 ....18 A2
Hawkins St *PRES* PR1 ....2 C1
Hawksbury Dr *PRES* PR1 ....23 H4
Hawkshead *PRES* PR1 ....24 A3
Hawkshead Av *CHLY/EC* PR7 ....43 B1
Hawkshead Rd *FUL/RIB* PR2 ....13 G3
Hawkswood *CHLY/EC* PR7 ....42 B4
Hawthorn Cl *KIRK/FR/WA* PR4 .....30 A2
    LEYL * PR25 ....34 D2
Hawthorn Crs *FUL/RIB* PR2 ....16 B2
Hawthorne Av *BER* PR5 ....26 C3
Hawthorne Cl *CHLYE* PR6 ....37 F1
Hawthorn Rd *FUL/RIB* PR2 ....12 C1
The Hawthorns *CHLY/EC* PR7 ....42 B3
    FUL/RIB PR2 ....12 B2
Haydock Av *LEYL* PR25 ....35 G4
Haydocks La *KIRK/FR/WA* PR4 ......10 B3
Haydock St *BER* * PR5 ....25 G4
Haydon Av *BER* PR5 ....31 G2
Hayfield Av *BER* PR5 ....27 E5
Hayfield Cl *BER* PR5 ....27 E5
Hayling Pl *FUL/RIB* PR2 ....11 E4
Haysworth St *PRES* PR1 ....18 B1
Haywood Cl *FUL/RIB* PR2 ....7 G5
Hazel Av *BER* PR5 ....26 A5
Hazel Cl *BER* PR5 ....25 H5
    PRES PR1 ....23 F3
Hazel Coppice *FUL/RIB* PR2 ....10 C5
Hazel Gv *BER* PR5 ....25 H5
    CHLYE PR6 ....40 C4
    FUL/RIB PR2 ....14 A4
    GAR/LONG PR3 ....15 C2
Hazelhurst Rd *FUL/RIB* PR2 ....20 A1
Hazelmere Rd *FUL/RIB* PR2 ....6 D5
    FUL/RIB PR2 ....17 E2
The Hazels *CHLY/EC* PR7 ....46 C4
Hazelwood Cl *LEYL* PR25 ....35 E3
Headley Rd *LEYL* PR25 ....35 E3
Heald House Rd *LEYL* PR25 ....36 A5
Heald St *CHLYE* PR6 ....45 E2
Heapey Rd *CHLYE* PR6 ....41 G4
Heather Cl *CHLYE* PR6 ....45 E2
Heather Gv *FUL/RIB* PR2 ....13 G5
Heatherleigh
    CROS/BRETH PR26 ....34 D2
The Heathers *BER* PR5 ....33 G5
Heatherway *FUL/RIB* PR2 ....13 G3
Heathfield Rd *FUL/RIB* PR2 ....13 G4
Heathrow Pl *CHLY/EC* PR7 ....44 A3
Heathway *FUL/RIB* PR2 ....12 B2
Heatley St *PRES* PR1 ....2 D4
    PRES PR1 ....2 E5

Heaton Cl *BER* PR5 ....25 F2
Heaton Mount Av *FUL/RIB* PR2 .....12 B1
Heaton Pl *PRES* PR1 ....19 G2
Heaton St *LEYL* PR25 ....35 E2
Hedgerows Rd
    CROS/BRETH PR26 ....34 A4
Hellifield Rd *FUL/RIB* PR2 ....12 A1
Helmsley Gn *LEYL* PR25 ....35 H2
Henderson St *PRES* PR1 ....18 A1
Hendon Pl *FUL/RIB* PR2 ....16 C1
Hennel La *BER* PR5 ....25 E3
Henrietta St *PRES* PR1 ....3 K2
Herbert St *LEYL* PR25 ....35 G2
    PRES PR1 ....3 J1
Hereford Gv *KIRK/FR/WA* PR4 ......10 B3
Hermon St *PRES* PR1 ....19 E2
Hern Av *BER* PR5 ....31 G1
Herschell St *PRES* PR1 ....3 H6
Hesketh Cl *PRES* PR1 ....19 G3
Hesketh Rd *FUL/RIB* PR2 ....19 H2
    GAR/LONG PR3 ....15 B2
Hesketh St *FUL/RIB* PR2 ....17 G2
Heversham Av *FUL/RIB* PR2 ....12 B1
Hewitt St *LEYL* PR25 ....35 H2
Hewlett St *CHLY/EC* PR7 ....46 B4
Hey End *KIRK/FR/WA* PR4 ....29 D1
The Heyes *CHLYE* PR6 ....37 F2
The Heys *CHLY/EC* PR7 ....46 D3
Heysham St *PRES* PR1 ....18 A2
Heywood Rd *FUL/RIB* PR2 ....16 C1
High Bank *CHLYE* PR6 ....41 G4
Higher Bank Rd *FUL/RIB* PR2 ....12 B5
Higher Cft *PRES* PR1 ....23 G4
Higher Furlong
    KIRK/FR/WA PR4 ....28 B4
Higher Greenfield *FUL/RIB* PR2 .....11 F3
Higher House La *CHLYE* PR6 ....41 G4
Higher Meadow *LEYL* PR25 ....36 C3
Higher Rd *GAR/LONG* PR3 ....15 C2
Higher Walton Rd *BER* PR5 ....25 G2
Highfield Av *BER* PR5 ....25 E5
    FUL/RIB PR2 ....13 E4
    LEYL PR25 ....36 A1
Highfield Dr *FUL/RIB* PR2 ....7 E5
    GAR/LONG PR3 ....15 C4
    KIRK/FR/WA PR4 ....28 B4
    PRES PR1 ....23 H4
Highfield Gv *BER* PR5 ....25 E5
Highfield Rd North
    CHLY/EC PR7 ....40 C5
Highfield Rd South
    CHLY/EC PR7 ....44 C1
Highgale Gdns *BER* PR5 ....32 A2
Highgate *PRES* PR1 ....23 F1
Highgate Av *FUL/RIB* PR2 ....12 A4
Highgate Cl *FUL/RIB* PR2 ....12 B4
High Gn *LEYL* PR25 ....35 F3
Highland Av *PRES* PR1 ....23 F2
High Meadow *BER* PR5 ....24 D4
Highrigg Dr *GAR/LONG* PR3 ....7 F4
High St *CHLY/EC* PR7 ....44 C2
    PRES PR1 ....3 G2
Highways Rd *CHLY/EC* PR7 ....43 B1
Hillbrook Rd *LEYL* PR25 ....35 F2
Hill Crest Av *FUL/RIB* PR2 ....7 E5
    GAR/LONG PR3 ....15 B3
Hillcrest Av *FUL/RIB* PR2 ....11 E4
Hillcrest Cft *GAR/LONG* PR3 ....15 B3
Hillcrest Dr *GAR/LONG* PR3 ....15 B3
Hill Cft *CHLYE* PR6 ....37 E2
Hillcroft *FUL/RIB* PR2 ....11 C1
Hillpark Av *BER* PR5 ....26 D5
    FUL/RIB PR2 ....11 H4
Hill Rd *LEYL* PR25 ....36 A3
    PRES PR1 ....23 C1
Hill Rd South *PRES* PR1 ....23 C3
The Hills *FUL/RIB* PR2 ....14 B1
Hillside Av *CROS/BRETH* PR26 .....31 F2
    FUL/RIB PR2 ....11 H4
Hillside Cl *CHLY/EC* PR7 ....43 A1
Hillside Crs *CHLYE* PR6 ....37 G4
Hillside Rd *BER* PR5 ....19 E5
Hill St *PRES* PR1 ....2 E3
Hill Top *KIRK/FR/WA* PR4 ....30 A3
Hill Top La *CHLYE* PR6 ....37 H4
Hill View Dr *CHLY/EC* PR7 ....46 B5
Hill Wk *LEYL* PR25 ....35 G2
Hindley Cl *FUL/RIB* PR2 ....13 E1
Hindley St *CHLY/EC* PR7 ....44 B4
Hind St *PRES* PR1 ....2 C6
Hodder Av *CHLY/EC* PR7 ....44 B5
Hodder Brook *FUL/RIB* PR2 ....14 A5
Hodder Cl *BER* PR5 ....32 D1
Hodder St *GAR/LONG* * PR3 ....15 C3
Hodson St *BER* PR5 ....25 G5
Hogg's La *CHLYE* PR6 ....45 F5
Hoghton La *BER* PR5 ....26 D3
Hoghton Rd *GAR/LONG* PR3 ....15 C3

    LEYL PR25 ....34 D3
Hoghton St *BER* PR5 ....31 G1
Hoghton Vw *PRES* PR1 ....19 E4
Holcombe Gv *CHLYE* PR6 ....45 E1
Holker Cl *BER* PR5 ....27 E3
Holland Av *BER* PR5 ....25 G4
Holland House Ct *BER* PR5 ....25 G3
Holland House Rd *BER* PR5 ....25 G3
Holland Rd *FUL/RIB* PR2 ....17 G2
Hollings *KIRK/FR/WA* PR4 ....29 D2
Hollinhead Crs *FUL/RIB* PR2 ....11 F4
Hollinhurst Av *PRES* PR1 ....17 G5
Hollins Gv *FUL/RIB* PR2 ....11 F5
Hollinshead St *CHLY/EC* PR7 ....44 C2
Hollins Rd *PRES* PR1 ....12 D5
Hollowforth La *KIRK/FR/WA* PR4 ...5 G1
Hollybank Cl *FUL/RIB* PR2 ....10 D3
Holly Cl *CHLYE* PR6 ....37 F2
Holly Crs *CHLY/EC* PR7 ....46 C2
Holly Gv *GAR/LONG* PR3 ....15 B2
Holly Pl *BER* PR5 ....33 F3
Hollywood Av *PRES* PR1 ....23 G3
Holman St *PRES* PR1 ....19 E2
Holme Rd *BER* PR5 ....32 B1
    PRES PR1 ....2 A5
    PRES PR1 ....16 C4
Holmes Ct *PRES* PR1 ....12 A5
Holme Slack La *PRES* PR1 ....13 E5
Holmes Meadow
    CROS/BRETH PR26 ....34 B3
Holmfield Crs *FUL/RIB* PR2 ....16 B3
Holmfield Rd *FUL/RIB* PR2 ....12 C4
Holmrook Rd *PRES* PR1 ....18 D2
Holsands Cl *FUL/RIB* PR2 ....13 G2
Holstein St *PRES* PR1 ....3 H2
Holt Av *CHLY/EC* PR7 ....46 D3
Holt Brow *LEYL* PR25 ....38 C1
Holt La *CHLYE* PR6 ....37 H1
Homestead *BER* PR5 ....33 F5
Homestead Cl *LEYL* PR25 ....34 D3
Honeysuckle Cl *CHLYE* PR6 ....40 B2
Honiton Wy *KIRK/FR/WA* PR4 ......10 D2
Hope St *CHLY/EC* PR7 ....44 C1
    PRES PR1 ....2 E3
Hopwood St *BER* PR5 ....32 C1
    PRES PR1 ....3 H2
Hornbeam Cl *PRES* PR1 ....23 F3
Hornby Av *FUL/RIB* PR2 ....13 C4
Hornby Cft *CROS/BRETH* PR26 .....34 B5
Hornby Rd *CHLYE* PR6 ....45 E4
    GAR/LONG PR3 ....15 C2
Hornchurch Dr *CHLY/EC* PR7 ....44 A2
Hornsea Cl *FUL/RIB* PR2 ....11 E4
Hough La *LEYL* PR25 ....35 G3
Houghton Cl *PRES* PR1 ....23 H3
Houghton Rd *PRES* PR1 ....23 G3
Houghton St *FUL/RIB* PR2 ....44 D2
Houldsworth Rd *FUL/RIB* PR2 ....12 A5
Howard Rd *CHLY/EC* PR7 ....44 B5
Howarth Rd *FUL/RIB* PR2 ....11 C5
Howe Gv *CHLY/EC* PR7 ....44 A3
The Howgills *FUL/RIB* PR2 ....12 C1
Howick Cross La *PRES* PR1 ....22 C1
Howick Moor La *PRES* PR1 ....22 D3
Howick Park Av *PRES* PR1 ....22 D2
Howick Park Cl *PRES* PR1 ....22 D2
Howick Park Dr *PRES* PR1 ....22 D2
Hoylake Cl *FUL/RIB* PR2 ....11 F2
Hoyles La *KIRK/FR/WA* PR4 ....10 A3
Hudson Ct *BER* PR5 ....33 C1
Hudson St *PRES* PR1 ....3 H5
Hugh Barn La *KIRK/FR/WA* PR4 ...29 C2
Hugh La *CROS/BRETH* PR26 ....34 D1
Hull St *FUL/RIB* PR2 ....17 G2
Humber St *GAR/LONG* PR3 ....15 B3
Hunniball Ct *FUL/RIB* PR2 ....17 C1
Hunters Fold *KIRK/FR/WA* PR4 .....28 C5
Hunters Ldg *BER* PR5 ....25 F3
Hunters Rd *LEYL* PR25 ....36 B3
Hunts Fld *CHLYE* PR6 ....37 E2
Hunt St *PRES* * PR1 ....2 B4
Hurn Gv *CHLY/EC* PR7 ....44 A3
Hurst Brook *CHLY/EC* PR7 ....46 D4
Hurst Pk *PRES* PR1 ....23 G2
Hurstway *FUL/RIB* PR2 ....11 H1
Hurstway Cl *FUL/RIB* PR2 ....11 H1
Hut La *CHLYE* PR6 ....45 H5
Hutton Hall Av *KIRK/FR/WA* PR4 ..22 C4

Iddesleigh Rd *PRES* * PR1 ....19 C3
Illingworth Rd *PRES* PR1 ....19 C3
Ilway *BER* PR5 ....25 F3
Ince La *CHLY/EC* PR7 ....42 C5
Ingleborough Wy *LEYL* PR25 ....36 A2

Ingle Cl *CHLYE* PR6 ....
Ingle Head *FUL/RIB* PR2 ....
Ingleton Rd *FUL/RIB* PR2 ....
Inglewhite Rd *GAR/LONG* PR3 ......
Ingot St *PRES* PR1 ....
Inkerman St *FUL/RIB* PR2 ....
Inskip Rd *FUL/RIB* PR2 ....
    LEYL PR25 ....
Intack Rd *KIRK/FR/WA* PR4 ....
Ipswich Rd *FUL/RIB* PR2 ....
Irongate *BER* PR5 ....
Ironside Cl *FUL/RIB* PR2 ....
Irvine St *PRES* PR1 ....
Irwell St *GAR/LONG* PR3 ....
Isabella St *GAR/LONG* PR3 ....
Isherwood St *PRES* PR1 ....
Isleworth Dr *CHLY/EC* PR7 ....
Ivy Bank *FUL/RIB* PR2 ....
Ivy Cl *LEYL* PR25 ....

J

Jackson Rd *CHLY/EC* * PR7 ....
    LEYL PR25 ....
Jackson St *BER* * PR5 ....
    CHLY/EC PR7 ....
Jacson St *PRES* PR1 ....
James Pl *CHLY/EC* PR7 ....
James St *BER* PR5 ....
    PRES PR1 ....
Jane La *CROS/BRETH* PR26 ....
Janice Dr *FUL/RIB* PR2 ....
Jasmine Rd *BER* PR5 ....
Jeffrey Av *GAR/LONG* PR3 ....
Jeffrey Hill Cl *FUL/RIB* PR2 ....
Jemmett St *PRES* PR1 ....
Johnspool *FUL/RIB* PR2 ....
John St *BER* PR5 ....
    CHLY/EC * PR7 ....
    LEYL PR25 ....
John William St *PRES* * PR1 ....
Jubilee Av *FUL/RIB* PR2 ....
Jubilee Pl *CHLYE* PR6 ....
Jubilee Rd *BER* PR5 ....
Judeland *CHLY/EC* PR7 ....
Junction Rd *PRES* PR1 ....
June's Wk *KIRK/FR/WA* PR4 ....
Juniper Cft *CHLYE* PR6 ....
Jutland St *PRES* PR1 ....

K

Kane St *FUL/RIB* PR2 ....
Kay St *PRES* * PR1 ....
Keats Cl *FUL/RIB* PR2 ....
Keats Wy *KIRK/FR/WA* PR4 ....
Kellet Acre *BER* PR5 ....
Kellet Av *LEYL* PR25 ....
Kellet La *BER* PR5 ....
Kellett St *CHLY/EC* * PR7 ....
Kem Mill La *CHLYE* PR6 ....
Kendal St *PRES* PR1 ....
Kenmure Pl *PRES* PR1 ....
Kennedy Av *PRES* PR1 ....
Kennington Rd *FUL/RIB* PR2 ....
Kensington Av *PRES* PR1 ....
Kensington Gdns *BER* PR5 ....
Kensington Gdns *CHLY/EC* PR7 .....
Kent Av *BER* * PR5 ....
Kent Dr *LEYL* PR25 ....
Kentmere Av *BER* PR5 ....
    LEYL PR25 ....
Kentmere Dr *KIRK/FR/WA* PR4 ......
Kent St *PRES* PR1 ....
Kerr Pl *PRES* PR1 ....
Kershaw St *CHLYE* PR6 ....
Kestor La *GAR/LONG* PR3 ....
Kestrel Cl *CHLYE* PR6 ....
Kew Gdns *LEYL* PR25 ....
    PRES PR1 ....
Kiddlington Cl *BER* PR5 ....
Kidsgrove *FUL/RIB* PR2 ....
Kilkerran Cl *CHLYE* PR6 ....
Kilmuir Cl *FUL/RIB* * PR2 ....
Kiln Cft *CHLYE* PR6 ....
Kilngate *BER* PR5 ....
Kilruddery Rd *PRES* PR1 ....
Kilsby Cl *BER* PR5 ....
Kilshaw St *PRES* PR1 ....
Kilworth Height *FUL/RIB* PR2 ....
Kimberley Rd *FUL/RIB* PR2 ....
Kimberley St *CHLY/EC* PR7 ....
Kingfisher St *PRES* PR1 ....

sbridge Cl PRES PR1 ...24 A5
s Ct LEYL PR25 ...35 G3
s Crs LEYL PR25 ...35 G3
s Cft BER PR5 ...25 F1
sdale Av FUL/RIB PR2 ...13 F3
sdale Cl BER PR5 ...25 H1
/L PR25 ...38 D1
s Dr FUL/RIB PR2 ...11 H3
sfold Dr PRES PR1 ...23 G4
shaven Dr PRES PR1 ...24 A5
sley Dr CHLY/EC PR7 ...44 A5
sley Rd KIRK/FR/WA PR4 ...10 C2
smead CHLY/EC PR7 ...44 C5
smuir Cl FUL/RIB * PR2 ...13 F4
St BER PR5 ...31 H2
LY/EC PR7 ...44 D4
R/LONG PR3 ...15 C3
/L PR25 ...35 G3
sway BER PR5 ...32 C1
LY/EC PR7 ...39 C5
RIB PR2 ...16 D1
/L PR25 ...35 E5
ES PR1 ...17 F5
sway Av GAR/LONG PR3 ...6 C2
sway West PRES PR1 ...23 E1
swood CHLY/EC PR7 ...44 B5
swood Rd LEYL PR25 ...35 G2
swood St PRES PR1 ...2 C4
y Av LEYL PR25 ...36 C3
am Cl LEYL PR25 ...34 D1
am St PRES PR1 ...2 D2
tall Cl CHLY/EC PR7 ...44 D5
tall Dr CHLY/EC PR7 ...44 D5
tall Rd CHLY/EC PR7 ...44 D5
wake Rd CHLYE PR6 ...41 G4
ngborne Brow BER PR5 ...26 A3
worth Cl CHLYE PR6 ...37 G2
Acre KIRK/FR/WA PR4 ...30 A1
La BER PR5 ...25 G1
vles St CHLY/EC PR7 ...44 C4
ES PR1 ...19 F3
vley Brow CHLYE PR6 ...41 E5
vsley Av LEYL PR25 ...32 A5
vsley Cl BER PR5 ...27 E4
vsley Dr BER PR5 ...27 F4
vsley Rd LEYL PR25 ...36 A4
vsley St PRES PR1 ...3 H5
a Rd FUL/RIB PR2 ...12 D3

L

rnum Av BER PR5 ...31 H1
rnum Cl PRES PR1 ...13 E5
rnum Dr FUL/RIB PR2 ...6 D5
rnum Rd CHLYE PR6 ...40 D4
Av PRES PR1 ...24 A4
Acre BER PR5 ...33 E1
Crosse Dr CHLYE PR6 ...40 C1
Hey Crs FUL/RIB PR2 ...16 A2
man St PRES PR1 ...2 C5
Pl BER PR5 ...25 G2
smith Rd FUL/RIB PR2 ...17 C1
St PRES PR1 ...3 F2
Well Dr FUL/RIB PR2 ...13 E1
well St PRES PR1 ...2 D3
land Gdns CHLY/EC PR7 ...44 A5
bert Cl FUL/RIB PR2 ...13 C5
bert Rd FUL/RIB PR2 ...13 C5
aster Av LEYL PR25 ...36 C3
astergate LEYL PR25 ...35 F4
aster La LEYL PR25 ...36 B3
aster Rd PRES PR1 ...3 F3
aster Rd North PRES PR1 ...3 F1
aster Rd CHLY/EC PR7 ...46 D4
La KIRK/FR/WA PR4 ...29 B3
aster St CHLY/EC PR7 ...46 D4
smoor Dr KIRK/FR/WA PR4 ...28 C2
cliffe Rd FUL/RIB PR2 ...13 C4
gdale Ct BER PR5 ...25 F5
gdale Crs FUL/RIB PR2 ...13 C5
gdale Gv CHLYE PR6 ...37 F5
gdale Rd FUL/RIB PR2 ...13 C5
R/LONG PR3 ...15 A4
YL PR25 ...38 D1
gden Crs BER PR5 ...32 D2
gden Dr FUL/RIB PR2 ...14 A5
gden Fold FUL/RIB PR2 ...9 H4
rfield Cl FUL/RIB PR2 ...7 F5
gholm Cl LEYL PR25 ...34 D4
gholme Rd PRES PR1 ...23 E2
gport Cl FUL/RIB PR2 ...7 F5
gton Brow CHLY/EC PR7 ...42 D4
R/LONG PR3 ...15 C3
gton Cl CHLY/EC PR7 ...42 D5
OS/BRETH PR26 ...34 C4

Langton St PRES PR1 ...2 B5
Lansborough Cl CROS/BRETH PR26 ...34 B4
Lansdown Hl FUL/RIB PR2 ...11 G1
Lappet Gv KIRK/FR/WA PR4 ...10 C3
Larch Av CHLYE PR6 ...41 E5
Larches La FUL/RIB PR2 ...16 D2
Larch Ga BER PR5 ...24 D2
Larchgate BER PR5 ...13 E1
Larch Gv BER PR5 ...25 H5
Larchway GAR/LONG PR3 ...15 C2
Larchwood FUL/RIB PR2 ...16 C2
PRES * PR1 ...23 F2
Larchwood Crs LEYL PR25 ...35 E5
Lark Av PRES PR1 ...24 A2
Larkfield CHLY/EC PR7 ...44 C2
Lark Hl BER PR5 ...26 B3
Larkhill Rd PRES PR1 ...3 J5
Larkhill St PRES PR1 ...3 G6
Latham St PRES PR1 ...2 C6
Latimer Dr KIRK/FR/WA PR4 ...29 D1
Lauderdale Rd FUL/RIB PR2 ...13 H4
Lauderdale St PRES PR1 ...2 C6
The Laund CROS/BRETH PR26 ...34 A3
Laurel Av CHLY/EC PR7 ...38 D4
Laurel Bank Av FUL/RIB PR2 ...11 C5
The Laurels CHLY/EC PR7 ...46 D2
Laurel St PRES PR1 ...3 H4
Lavender Cl FUL/RIB PR2 ...13 E2
Lavender Gv CHLY/EC PR7 ...44 C5
Lawnwood Av CHLY/EC PR7 ...44 A5
Lawrence Av BER PR5 ...25 H4
Lawrence La CHLY/EC PR7 ...42 C3
Lawrence Rd CHLY/EC PR7 ...44 A5
PRES * PR1 ...23 F1
Lawrence St FUL/RIB PR2 ...11 H5
Lawson St CHLYE PR6 ...45 E2
PRES PR1 ...3 F2
Laxey Gv PRES PR1 ...13 F5
Layton Rd FUL/RIB PR2 ...16 B2
Leach Pl BER PR5 ...33 F1
Leadale FUL/RIB PR2 ...16 A1
Leadale Gn LEYL PR25 ...34 D3
Leadale Rd LEYL PR25 ...34 D3
Leafy Cl LEYL PR25 ...35 H5
Leagram Crs FUL/RIB PR2 ...13 H3
Lea Rd CHLYE PR6 ...40 C2
KIRK/FR/WA PR4 ...10 C5
Leek St PRES PR1 ...19 G3
Leesands Cl FUL/RIB PR2 ...16 B1
Leeson Av CHLY/EC PR7 ...46 B1
Lee St GAR/LONG PR3 ...15 A3
Leeward Rd FUL/RIB PR2 ...16 D3
Leicester Rd PRES PR1 ...18 B2
Leigh Brow PRES PR1 ...24 D4
Leigh House Ctyd BER * PR5 ...25 E3
Leigh Rw CHLY/EC PR7 ...44 C3
Leighton St PRES PR1 ...2 C2
Lennon St CHLY/EC PR7 ...44 B5
Lennox St PRES PR1 ...3 G5
Leo Case Ct PRES PR1 ...19 F3
Letchworth Dr CHLY/EC PR7 ...44 B4
Letchworth Wks CHLY/EC PR7 ...44 B4
Levens Dr LEYL PR25 ...36 B2
Levensgarth Av FUL/RIB PR2 ...7 F5
Levens St PRES PR1 ...19 F2
Lever House La LEYL PR25 ...36 A2
Lex St PRES PR1 ...19 E3
Leyburn Cl FUL/RIB PR2 ...13 C3
Leyfield PRES PR1 ...23 H4
Leyfield Rd LEYL PR25 ...35 F3
Leyland La LEYL PR25 ...34 D5
Leyland Rd PRES PR1 ...2 A7
PRES PR1 ...24 A3
Leyland Wy LEYL PR25 ...36 A3
Leyton Av LEYL PR25 ...34 D5
Library Rd CHLYE PR6 ...33 F5
Library St CHLY/EC PR7 ...44 C3
PRES PR1 ...3 G4
Lichen Cl CHLY/EC PR7 ...46 B1
Lichfield Rd CHLY/EC PR7 ...44 C4
FUL/RIB PR2 ...16 D1
Lidget Av FUL/RIB PR2 ...16 A2
Liege Rd LEYL PR25 ...35 G4
Lightfoot Cl GAR/LONG PR3 ...6 D5
Lightfoot Green La KIRK/FR/WA PR4 ...6 B5
Lightfoot La FUL/RIB PR2 ...11 F1
FUL/RIB PR2 ...11 F1
KIRK/FR/WA PR4 ...10 D1
Lighthurst Av CHLY/EC PR7 ...44 C5
Lighthurst La CHLY/EC PR7 ...44 D5
Lilac Av PRES PR1 ...24 B4
Lilac Gv PRES PR1 ...13 E5
Lily Gv PRES PR1 ...13 E5
Limbrick Rd CHLYE PR6 ...45 E3

Lime Cha GAR/LONG PR3 ...6 C5
Lime Cl PRES PR1 ...23 E2
Lime Gv CHLY/EC PR7 ...44 C5
FUL/RIB PR2 ...16 D1
GAR/LONG PR3 ...15 B2
Limes Av CHLY/EC PR7 ...39 E3
Lincoln Cha FUL/RIB PR2 ...16 A2
Lincoln St PRES PR1 ...3 J1
Lincoln Wk PRES * PR1 ...3 J1
Lindale Rd FUL/RIB PR2 ...12 C4
GAR/LONG PR3 ...15 A5
Linden Av BER PR5 ...24 D5
Linden Dr BER PR5 ...24 D5
Linden Gv CHLYE PR6 ...40 D4
FUL/RIB PR2 ...13 G5
Lindle Av KIRK/FR/WA PR4 ...22 C4
Lindle Cl KIRK/FR/WA PR4 ...22 C4
Lindle Crs KIRK/FR/WA PR4 ...22 C4
Lindle La KIRK/FR/WA PR4 ...22 C4
Lindley St BER PR5 ...31 H1
Lindsay Av LEYL PR25 ...35 H3
Lindsay Dr CHLY/EC PR7 ...44 A3
Lingwell Cl CHLYE PR6 ...40 C2
Links Fld FUL/RIB PR2 ...11 G5
Links Ga FUL/RIB PR2 ...11 G5
Links Rd PRES PR1 ...17 F5
Linnet St PRES PR1 ...18 D1
Linton Gv PRES PR1 ...23 F1
Linton St FUL/RIB PR2 ...11 H5
Liptrott Rd CHLY/EC PR7 ...44 A5
Little Acre KIRK/FR/WA PR4 ...28 C2
Little Banks Cl BER * PR5 ...33 F3
Little Carr La CHLY/EC PR7 ...44 D5
Little Cl PRES PR1 ...23 C3
Little La GAR/LONG PR3 ...15 B3
Little Twining KIRK/FR/WA PR4 ...28 C3
Liverpool Old Rd KIRK/FR/WA PR4 ...28 B4
Liverpool Rd KIRK/FR/WA PR4 ...22 C3
KIRK/FR/WA PR4 ...28 B4
PRES PR1 ...2 A7
PRES PR1 ...23 E1
Livesey St PRES PR1 ...3 K5
Lockhart St PRES PR1 ...18 B1
Lockside Rd FUL/RIB PR2 ...16 D3
Lodge Cl BER PR5 ...25 H5
Lodge La CROS/BRETH PR26 ...31 E3
Lodge St PRES PR1 ...3 J3
Lodge Vw GAR/LONG * PR3 ...15 B4
KIRK/FR/WA PR4 ...31 E2
The Lodgings FUL/RIB PR2 ...13 E2
London Rd PRES PR1 ...3 K4
London Wy BER PR5 ...25 E3
Long Acre BER PR5 ...33 G4
Longbrook Av BER PR5 ...25 G4
Long Butts PRES PR1 ...24 D4
Long Cl CROS/BRETH PR26 ...34 A4
Long Copse CHLY/EC PR7 ...43 D1
Long Cft KIRK/FR/WA PR4 ...28 C3
Long Croft Meadow CHLY/EC PR7 ...40 B5
Longfield FUL/RIB PR2 ...7 F5
PRES PR1 ...7 F5
Longfield Av CHLY/EC PR7 ...46 C3
Longfield Mnr CHLY/EC PR7 ...46 C3
Longley Cl FUL/RIB PR2 ...7 F5
Long Meadow CHLY/EC PR7 ...44 A5
Longmeanygate CROS/BRETH PR26 ...34 A2
Long Moss CROS/BRETH PR26 ...34 A4
Long Moss La KIRK/FR/WA PR4 ...29 C3
Long Moss Mdw KIRK/FR/WA PR4 ...29 D3
Longridge Rd FUL/RIB PR2 ...13 H4
Longsands La FUL/RIB PR2 ...13 E3
Longton By-Pass KIRK/FR/WA PR4 ...22 C4
KIRK/FR/WA PR4 ...28 C4
Longton St CHLYE PR6 ...44 C3
Longworth Av CHLY/EC PR7 ...46 D3
Longworth St BER PR5 ...25 G4
CHLY/EC PR7 ...44 B4
PRES PR1 ...19 E2
Lonsdale Cha BER * PR5 ...31 H2
Lonsdale Cl LEYL PR25 ...38 C1
Lonsdale Ms BER * PR5 ...31 H2
Lonsdale Rd PRES PR1 ...18 C4
Lord's Av BER PR5 ...31 H2
Lords Cft CHLYE PR6 ...37 E2
Lord's La PRES PR1 ...24 A5
Lord St CHLY/EC PR7 ...42 C5
CHLYE PR6 ...4 D3
PRES PR1 ...3 G3
Lord's Wk PRES PR1 ...3 H3
Lorne St CHLY/EC PR7 ...44 C3
Lorraine Av FUL/RIB PR2 ...12 B1
Lorton Cl FUL/RIB PR2 ...12 B2
Lostock Ct BER * PR5 ...31 H2

Lostock La BER PR5 ...32 A2
Lostock Meadow CHLYE PR6 ...37 E3
Lostock Sq BER PR5 ...31 H2
Lostock Vw BER PR5 ...31 G2
Lourdes Av BER PR5 ...24 C5
Lovat Rd PRES PR1 ...18 B1
Lowcroft FUL/RIB PR2 ...6 B2
Lower Bank Rd FUL/RIB PR2 ...12 B5
Lower Burgh Rd CHLY/EC PR7 ...47 E1
Lower Burgh Wy CHLY/EC PR7 ...47 E1
Lower Fld CROS/BRETH PR26 ...31 F3
Lower Greenfield FUL/RIB PR2 ...11 F4
Lower Hey KIRK/FR/WA PR4 ...28 C1
Lower House Rd LEYL PR25 ...34 D4
Lower La GAR/LONG PR3 ...15 C4
Lowesby Cl BER PR5 ...25 G3
Low Gn LEYL PR25 ...35 F3
Lowick Cl BER PR5 ...27 E2
Lowood Gv FUL/RIB PR2 ...16 B2
Lowry Cl BER PR5 ...31 G2
Lowther Crs CROS/BRETH PR26 ...34 D2
Lowther Dr CROS/BRETH PR26 ...34 D2
Lowther St FUL/RIB PR2 ...17 G2
Lowthian St PRES PR1 ...3 F3
Lowthorpe Crs PRES PR1 ...18 D1
Lowthorpe Rd PRES PR1 ...18 D1
Loxley Gn FUL/RIB PR2 ...13 E2
Lucas Av CHLY/EC PR7 ...43 B3
Lucas La CHLYE PR6 ...40 C1
Lucerne Rd FUL/RIB PR2 ...13 E4
Lulworth Av FUL/RIB PR2 ...17 H1
Lulworth Pl BER PR5 ...25 F5
Lulworth Rd FUL/RIB * PR2 ...12 C4
Lund St PRES PR1 ...3 F2
Lune Dr LEYL PR25 ...36 C2
Lune St GAR/LONG PR3 ...15 C2
PRES PR1 ...2 E4
Lupin Cl CHLYE PR6 ...40 B2
Lupton St CHLY/EC PR7 ...44 C5
Luton Rd FUL/RIB PR2 ...16 C1
Lutwidge Av PRES PR1 ...19 E2
Lychfield BER PR5 ...32 C2
Lychgate PRES PR1 ...3 H3
Lydd Gv CHLY/EC PR7 ...44 A3
Lydgate CHLY/EC PR7 ...44 A5
Lydiate La CHLY/EC PR7 ...42 B1
LEYL PR25 ...32 A5
Lydric Av BER PR5 ...27 E4
Lyndale Av BER PR5 ...25 E5
Lyndale Cl LEYL PR25 ...38 D1
Lyndale Gv BER PR5 ...25 E4
Lyndeth Cl FUL/RIB PR2 ...13 G2
Lyndhurst Dr FUL/RIB PR2 ...16 C1
Lynn Pl FUL/RIB * PR2 ...19 F1
Lynton Av LEYL PR25 ...36 A4
Lynwood Av FUL/RIB PR2 ...9 G4
Lyons La CHLY/EC PR7 ...44 D3
Lyons La South CHLY/EC PR7 ...44 D3
Lytham Rd FUL/RIB PR2 ...11 G5
Lytham St CHLYE PR6 ...45 E3
Lythcoe Av FUL/RIB PR2 ...11 G4

M

Mackay Cft CHLYE PR6 ...44 D2
Mackenzie Cl CHLYE PR6 ...44 D2
Maddy St PRES PR1 ...2 A2
Mafeking Rd FUL/RIB PR2 ...17 G1
Magnolia Cl FUL/RIB PR2 ...13 E2
Magnolia Dr LEYL PR25 ...36 C2
Magnolia St PRES PR1 ...23 F3
Main Sprit Weind PRES PR1 ...3 G4
Mainway Ct BER * PR5 ...32 C1
Maitland Cl PRES PR1 ...19 E3
Maitland St PRES PR1 ...19 F3
Malcolm St PRES PR1 ...19 F2
Malden St LEYL PR25 ...35 G3
Maldon Pl FUL/RIB * PR2 ...19 F1
Malham Pl FUL/RIB PR2 ...19 F1
The Mall FUL/RIB PR2 ...19 G1
Mallard Cl LEYL PR25 ...34 C4
Mallards Wk BER PR5 ...33 E4
Mallom Av CHLY/EC PR7 ...43 C1
Malthouse Ct FUL/RIB PR2 ...2 B1
Malthouse Wy PRES PR1 ...23 H3
The Maltings KIRK/FR/WA PR4 ...28 B2
Malton Dr BER PR5 ...31 G2
Malvern Av PRES PR1 ...24 D1
Malvern Cl BER PR5 ...32 A1
Malvern Rd PRES PR1 ...3 K7
Malvern St PRES PR1 ...24 D1
Manby Cl BER PR5 ...27 F3
Manchester Rd PRES PR1 ...3 H4
Manning Rd PRES PR1 ...19 G2
Manor Av FUL/RIB PR2 ...12 D4
PRES PR1 ...23 F2

Manor Cl BER PR5 ...... 27 F3
Manor Ct FUL/RIB PR2 ...... 11 F1
Manorcroft KIRK/FR/WA PR4 ...... 28 B2
Manor Gv PRES PR1 ...... 23 E2
Manor House Cl
  CROS/BRETH PR26 ...... 34 B4
Manor House Crs PRES PR1 ...... 12 D5
Manor House La PRES PR1 ...... 12 D5
Manor La PRES PR1 ...... 23 F2
Manor Pk PRES PR1 ...... 13 E5
Manor Rd FUL/RIB PR6 ...... 37 F1
Mansfield Dr BER 27 E3
Manston Gv CHLY/EC PR7 ...... 44 A3
Maplebank FUL/RIB PR2 ...... 16 A2
Maple Crs PRES PR1 ...... 2 C5
Maple Dr BER PR5 ...... 25 H5
Maple Gv CHLYE PR6 ...... 40 D4
  FUL/RIB PR2 ...... 9 H4
  FUL/RIB PR2 ...... 14 A4
  PRES PR1 ...... 23 F2
Maplewood Cl LEYL PR25 ...... 35 E4
Marathon Pl CROS/BRETH PR26 ...... 34 C1
Mardale Crs LEYL PR25 ...... 35 H5
Mardale Rd GAR/LONG PR3 ...... 15 A5
  PRES PR1 ...... 20 A2
Maresfield Rd PRES PR1 ...... 23 H1
Marewood CHLY/EC PR7 ...... 40 B5
Margaret Rd PRES PR1 ...... 24 A2
Margaret St PRES PR1 ...... 3 G2
Margate Rd FUL/RIB PR2 ...... 11 E4
Marilyn Av BER PR5 ...... 31 H1
Marina Cl BER PR5 ...... 24 C5
Marina Dr BER PR5 ...... 24 C5
  FUL/RIB PR2 ...... 12 A1
Marina Gv BER PR5 ...... 24 C5
Mariners Wy FUL/RIB PR2 ...... 17 E3
Maritime Wy FUL/RIB PR2 ...... 16 D4
Mark Cl PRES PR1 ...... 24 B5
Market Hall PRES * PR1 ...... 3 F3
Market Pl GAR/LONG PR3 ...... 15 C3
  PRES PR1 ...... 3 F4
Market St CHLY/EC PR7 ...... 44 C2
  PRES PR1 ...... 3 F3
Market St West PRES PR1 ...... 2 E3
Markham St FUL/RIB PR2 ...... 17 G2
Markland St PRES PR1 ...... 2 D5
Mark's Av CROS/BRETH PR26 ...... 31 E4
Marl Av PRES PR1 ...... 23 F2
Marlborough Dr BER PR5 ...... 25 E2
  FUL/RIB PR2
Marlborough St CHLYE PR6 ...... 45 E1
Marl Cft PRES PR1 ...... 23 H4
Marlfield Cl FUL/RIB PR2 ...... 10 D2
Marl Hill Crs FUL/RIB PR2 ...... 20 A1
Marron Cl LEYL PR25 ...... 35 E3
Marsden Cl CHLY/EC PR7 ...... 42 B3
Marsett Pl FUL/RIB PR2 ...... 13 G3
Marshall Gv FUL/RIB PR2 ...... 11 E4
Marshall's Brow PRES PR1 ...... 24 A3
Marshall's Ct PRES PR1 ...... 24 A2
Marsh La KIRK/FR/WA PR4 ...... 28 B2
  PRES PR1 ...... 2 B4
Marsh Wy PRES PR1 ...... 23 G4
Marston Cl FUL/RIB PR2 ...... 11 G1
Marston Moor FUL/RIB PR2 ...... 11 G1
Martinfield FUL/RIB PR2 ...... 7 F5
Martin Field Rd PRES PR1 ...... 23 H4
Marton Rd FUL/RIB PR2 ...... 16 D3
Marybank Cl FUL/RIB PR2 ...... 13 G2
Mary St West GAR/LONG PR3 ...... 15 B2
Masefield Pl BER PR5 ...... 25 F4
Masonfield BER PR5 ...... 33 F4
Mason Hill Vw FUL/RIB PR2 ...... 12 C4
Mason House Crs FUL/RIB * PR2 ...... 11 E3
Mason St CHLYE PR6 ...... 41 E5
Masonwood FUL/RIB PR2 ...... 12 C2
Matlock Pl FUL/RIB PR2 ...... 11 E3
Matterdale Rd LEYL PR25 ...... 35 H5
Maudland Bank PRES PR1 ...... 2 C1
Maudland Rd PRES PR1 ...... 2 D1
Maud St CHLY/EC PR7 ...... 44 B4
Maureen Av BER PR5 ...... 31 H1
Mavis Dr CHLY/EC PR7 ...... 46 C4
Mayfield Av BER PR5 ...... 32 A1
  FUL/RIB PR2 ...... 11 E3
Mayfield Rd CHLYE PR6 ...... 44 D1
  FUL/RIB PR2 ...... 17 F2
  LEYL PR25 ...... 35 G5
Mayflower Av PRES PR1 ...... 23 E2
Maynard St FUL/RIB PR2 ...... 17 H1
Maypark BER PR5 ...... 33 E4
McKenzie St BER PR5 ...... 32 D1
Mead Av LEYL PR25 ...... 35 H4
Meadoway KIRK/FR/WA PR4 ...... 28 B2
Meadow Bank PRES PR1 ...... 23 G3
Meadowbarn Cl
  KIRK/FR/WA PR4 ...... 10 C3
Meadow Ct PRES PR1 ...... 2 C7

Meadowcroft CHLY/EC PR7 ...... 38 D4
Meadowcroft Rd LEYL PR25 ...... 34 D5
Meadowfield FUL/RIB PR2 ...... 12 B1
Meadow Fld PRES PR1 ...... 24 A4
Meadow Head La
  KIRK/FR/WA PR4 ...... 28 B3
Meadowland Cl
  CROS/BRETH PR26 ...... 35 E1
Meadowlands CHLY/EC PR7 ...... 46 B1
Meadow La BER PR5 ...... 33 F5
Meadow Reach PRES PR1 ...... 23 F4
The Meadows BER * PR5 ...... 25 H4
Meadowside KIRK/FR/WA PR4 ...... 28 C5
Meadowside Dr BER PR5 ...... 27 E5
  CROS/BRETH PR26 ...... 34 B4
Meadow St LEYL PR25 ...... 35 G3
  PRES PR1 ...... 3 H2
Meadow V CROS/BRETH PR26 ...... 34 A4
Meadow Wy CHLY/EC PR7 ...... 46 B5
Meads Rd FUL/RIB PR2 ...... 17 F2
Meadway CHLYE PR6 ...... 37 F1
  PRES PR1 ...... 23 E1
Mealhouse La CHLY/EC PR7 ...... 44 C2
Meanygate BER PR5 ...... 32 C1
Mearley Rd FUL/RIB PR2 ...... 13 G4
Meath Rd PRES PR1 ...... 23 H1
Medway FUL/RIB PR2 ...... 12 B2
Medway Cl BER PR5 ...... 24 D5
Melba Rd FUL/RIB PR2 ...... 13 G5
Melbert Av FUL/RIB PR2 ...... 11 F5
Melbourne St PRES PR1 ...... 3 F2
Melford Cl CHLYE PR6 ...... 41 E4
Mellings PRES PR1 ...... 19 E5
Mellings Fold PRES * PR1 ...... 19 E5
Melling St PRES PR1 ...... 3 F2
Mellor Ct GAR/LONG PR3 ...... 15 C3
Mellor Pl PRES * PR1 ...... 3 K5
Mellor Rd LEYL PR25 ...... 34 D2
Melrose Av FUL/RIB PR2 ...... 13 E3
Melrose Wy CHLY/EC PR7 ...... 44 D4
Melton Pl LEYL PR25 ...... 35 H2
Menai Dr FUL/RIB PR2 ...... 11 H1
Mendip Rd LEYL PR25 ...... 36 B3
Mercer Rd BER PR5 ...... 24 C5
Mercer St PRES PR1 ...... 19 E3
Mere Cl GAR/LONG PR3 ...... 6 C2
Merefield CHLY/EC PR7 ...... 44 A1
Mere Fold CHLY/EC PR7 ...... 46 B2
Mereside Cl KIRK/FR/WA PR4 ...... 28 B3
Merlin Cl CHLYE PR6 ...... 41 G4
Merlin Gv LEYL PR25 ...... 34 D5
Merrick Av PRES PR1 ...... 19 H3
Merryburn Cl FUL/RIB PR2 ...... 12 C4
Merry Trees La KIRK/FR/WA PR4 ...... 10 C3
Mersey St FUL/RIB PR2 ...... 17 G3
  GAR/LONG PR3 ...... 15 B3
Merton Av FUL/RIB PR2 ...... 12 B3
Merton Gv CHLYE PR6 ...... 41 E4
Mete St PRES PR1 ...... 19 F3
Methuen Av BER PR5 ...... 27 E3
  FUL/RIB PR2 ...... 12 A2
Methuen Cl BER PR5 ...... 27 E3
Methuen Dr BER PR5 ...... 27 F3
Mickleden Av FUL/RIB PR2 ...... 12 B1
Middlefield CROS/BRETH PR26 ...... 34 A4
Middleforth Gn PRES PR1 ...... 24 A2
Middlewood Cl CHLY/EC PR7 ...... 42 C4
Midge Hall La KIRK/FR/WA PR4 ...... 29 D5
Midgery La FUL/RIB PR2 ...... 7 C5
  FUL/RIB PR2 ...... 13 E2
Milbeck Cl GAR/LONG PR3 ...... 15 A5
Miles Ct PRES PR1 ...... 18 B1
Mile Stone Meadow CHLYE PR6 ...... 39 F3
Miles Wk PRES PR1 ...... 18 A1
Millbank FUL/RIB PR2 ...... 11 G5
Millbrook Wy PRES PR1 ...... 23 G4
Mill Cl GAR/LONG PR3 ...... 15 C2
Millcroft FUL/RIB PR2 ...... 11 G4
Miller Ar PRES PR1 ...... 3 G4
Miller Fld FUL/RIB PR2 ...... 10 C5
Miller La KIRK/FR/WA PR4 ...... 4 A1
  KIRK/FR/WA PR4 ...... 10 C3
Miller Rd PRES PR1 ...... 19 F2
Millersgate KIRK/FR/WA PR4 ...... 10 C4
Miller St PRES PR1 ...... 19 E3
Millfield Rd CHLY/EC PR7 ...... 44 B1
Mill Ga FUL/RIB PR2 ...... 11 H5
Mill Hvn FUL/RIB PR2 ...... 11 H5
Mill Hl PRES PR1 ...... 2 D2
Mill La BER PR5 ...... 25 F1
  CHLY/EC PR7 ...... 46 C3
  CHLYE PR6 ...... 37 G3
  CROS/BRETH PR26 ...... 35 E1
  FUL/RIB PR2 ...... 11 G4
  LEYL PR25 ...... 34 D4
Mill St CHLY/EC PR7 ...... 46 C4
  LEYL PR25 ...... 34 D4
  LEYL PR25 ...... 35 H1

  PRES * PR1 ...... 2 B3
Millwood Gld CHLY/EC PR7 ...... 44 B1
Millwood Rd BER PR5 ...... 24 D3
Milner St PRES PR1 ...... 18 B1
Milton Cl BER PR5 ...... 25 F4
Milton Rd CHLY/EC PR7 ...... 46 C5
Milton Ter CHLYE PR6 ...... 40 D5
Mimosa Cl CHLY/EC PR7 ...... 40 A4
Mimosa Rd FUL/RIB PR2 ...... 19 G1
Minster Pk KIRK/FR/WA PR4 ...... 10 C3
Mintholme Av BER PR5 ...... 27 E4
Mitton Dr FUL/RIB PR2 ...... 14 A5
Moira Crs FUL/RIB PR2 ...... 13 G4
Molyneux Ct PRES PR1 ...... 3 H3
Mona Pl PRES PR1 ...... 2 C3
Monks Dr GAR/LONG PR3 ...... 15 B4
Monks Wk PRES PR1 ...... 17 G5
Montcliffe Rd CHLYE PR6 ...... 45 E1
Montgomery St BER PR5 ...... 32 D1
Montjoly St PRES * PR1 ...... 19 E4
Montrose Cl CHLYE PR6 ...... 45 E4
Moon St BER PR5 ...... 32 C1
Moor Av PRES PR1 ...... 22 D2
Moorbrook St PRES PR1 ...... 18 A2
Moorcroft KIRK/FR/WA PR4 ...... 6 B3
Moorcroft Crs FUL/RIB PR2 ...... 13 F5
Moore St PRES PR1 ...... 19 E4
Moor Fld KIRK/FR/WA PR4 ...... 29 D2
Moorfield Cl FUL/RIB PR2 ...... 7 E5
  PRES PR1 ...... 23 E3
Moorfield Dr FUL/RIB PR2 ...... 13 G5
Moorfield Rd LEYL PR25 ...... 34 C4
Moorfields CHLYE PR6 ...... 45 E1
Moorfields Av FUL/RIB PR2 ...... 7 E5
Moorgate FUL/RIB PR2 ...... 12 B3
Moor Hall St PRES PR1 ...... 18 A1
Moorhey Crs BER PR5 ...... 33 E1
  PRES PR1 ...... 23 F1
Moorhey Dr PRES PR1 ...... 23 F1
The Moorings CHLYE PR6 ...... 45 E2
Moorland Av FUL/RIB PR2 ...... 13 F3
Moorland Crs FUL/RIB PR2 ...... 13 F4
Moorland Ga CHLYE PR6 ...... 45 E4
Moor La KIRK/FR/WA PR4 ...... 22 B5
  PRES PR1 ...... 2 E1
Moor Park Av PRES PR1 ...... 18 C1
Moor Park Ct PRES * PR1 ...... 18 B1
Moor Rd CHLY/EC PR7 ...... 44 A5
Moorside Av FUL/RIB PR2 ...... 13 H5
Moorside Dr PRES PR1 ...... 23 F3
Moorside La KIRK/FR/WA PR4 ...... 5 E1
Morland Av BER PR5 ...... 31 G2
Morley Cft CROS/BRETH PR26 ...... 35 E1
Mornington Rd PRES PR1 ...... 19 H2
  PRES * PR1 ...... 23 F1
Morris Cl LEYL PR25 ...... 35 G4
Morris Ct FUL/RIB * PR2 ...... 19 F1
Morris Crs FUL/RIB PR2 ...... 19 F1
Morrison St CHLYE PR6 ...... 40 D5
Morris Rd CHLY * PR6 ...... 45 E1
  FUL/RIB PR2 ...... 19 F1
Mosley St LEYL PR25 ...... 35 G3
  PRES PR1 ...... 19 E3
Moss Acre Rd PRES PR1 ...... 24 A3
Moss Av FUL/RIB PR2 ...... 17 E1
Moss Bank CHLY/EC PR7 ...... 46 C4
Moss Bridge Pk BER PR5 ...... 31 H1
Mossbrook Dr KIRK/FR/WA PR4 ...... 10 C3
Moss Cl CHLYE PR6 ...... 45 E2
Mossfield Cl BER PR5 ...... 31 H1
Mossfield Rd CHLYE PR6 ...... 45 E2
Moss House Rd KIRK/FR/WA PR4 ...... 6 B3
Mosslands LEYL PR25 ...... 34 D3
Moss La BER PR5 ...... 31 H1
  CHLY/EC PR7 ...... 46 C4
  CHLYE PR6 ...... 40 D4
  CROS/BRETH PR26 ...... 30 D4
  KIRK/FR/WA PR4 ...... 4 A1
  KIRK/FR/WA PR4 ...... 29 C2
  LEYL PR25 ...... 36 A2
Moss Side Wy
  CROS/BRETH PR26 ...... 34 B5
Moss St BER PR5 ...... 31 H1
  PRES * PR1 ...... 2 D2
Mossway KIRK/FR/WA PR4 ...... 29 D3
Mottram Cl CHLYE PR6 ...... 40 C1
Mounsey Rd BER PR5 ...... 32 D1
Mountain Rd CHLY/EC PR7 ...... 46 C5
Mountbatten Cl FUL/RIB PR2 ...... 17 F3
Mountbatten Rd CHLY/EC PR7 ...... 44 A4
Mount Pleasant CHLYE PR6 ...... 37 G4
Mount St PRES PR1 ...... 2 E5
Muirfield PRES PR1 ...... 17 E5
Muirfield Cl FUL/RIB PR2 ...... 11 F2
Mulberry Av PRES PR1 ...... 23 E3
Mulgrave Av FUL/RIB PR2 ...... 17 E2
Muncaster Rd PRES PR1 ...... 18 B1
Munro Crs FUL/RIB PR2 ...... 13 G5

Murdock Av FUL/RIB PR2 1
Murray Av CROS/BRETH PR26 3
Murray St LEYL PR25 3
  PRES PR1 1
Mythop Pl FUL/RIB PR2 1

N

Nab Rd CHLYE PR6 4
Naptha La CROS/BRETH PR26 3
Nares St LEYL PR25 3
Nateby Cl GAR/LONG PR3 3
Nateby Pl FUL/RIB PR2 1
Navigation Wy FUL/RIB PR2 1
Neapsands Cl FUL/RIB PR2 1
Neargates CHLY/EC PR7 4
Nell La LEYL PR25 3
Nelson Av LEYL PR25 3
Nelson Crs FUL/RIB PR2 1
Nelson Dr FUL/RIB PR2 1
Nelson Rd CHLY/EC PR7 4
Nelson St BER PR5 3
Nelson Ter PRES * PR1
Nelson Wy FUL/RIB PR2 1
Nene Cl LEYL PR25 3
Neston St PRES PR1 1
Netherley Rd CHLY/EC PR7 4
Nevett St PRES PR1 1
Neville St GAR/LONG PR3
Newark Pl FUL/RIB PR2 3
New Brook Houses PRES * PR1 1
Newbury Cl FUL/RIB PR2
Newbury Gn FUL/RIB PR2
Newby Dr LEYL PR25 3
Newby Pl FUL/RIB PR2 1
New Cock Yd PRES PR1
Newfield Rd BER PR5 3
Newgate FUL/RIB PR2 1
Newgate La KIRK/FR/WA PR4 3
New Hall La PRES PR1
Newlands CHLY/EC PR7 4
Newlands Av PRES PR1 2
New La PRES PR1 2
New Links Av FUL/RIB PR2 1
Newlyn Pl FUL/RIB PR2 1
New Market St CHLY/EC PR7 4
New Mill St CHLY/EC PR7 4
New Moss La CHLYE PR6 4
New Preston Ml PRES * PR1
New Rd BER PR5 2
  CHLY/EC PR7 4
New Rough Hey FUL/RIB PR2 1
Newsham Hall La
  KIRK/FR/WA PR4
Newsham St FUL/RIB * PR2
Newsome St LEYL PR25 3
New St CHLY/EC PR7 4
Newton Av PRES PR1 1
Newton Cl CROS/BRETH PR26 3
Newton Ct FUL/RIB PR2 1
Newton Rd FUL/RIB PR2 1
Newton St PRES PR1 1
Nib La PRES PR1 4
Nichol St CHLY/EC * PR7 4
Nimes St PRES PR1 1
Nine Elms FUL/RIB PR2 1
Noel Sq FUL/RIB * PR2 1
Nook Crs FUL/RIB PR2
Nookfield CROS/BRETH PR26 3
Nook Gld FUL/RIB PR2
Nooklands FUL/RIB PR2 1
Nook La BER PR5 3
Noor St PRES PR1
Norbreck Dr FUL/RIB PR2 1
Norcross Pl FUL/RIB PR2 1
Norfolk Cl LEYL PR25
Norfolk Rd BER PR5 2
  PRES PR1
Normandy Rd KIRK/FR/WA PR4 6
Norris St CHLY/EC PR7 4
  FUL/RIB PR2 1
  PRES PR1 1
Northbrook Rd LEYL PR25 35
North Cliff St PRES PR1 2
Northcote Rd PRES PR1 2
Northcote St LEYL PR25 35
Northenden Rd CHLY/EC PR7 46
Northgate LEYL PR25 3
Northgate Dr CHLYE PR6 41
North Gv BER PR5 3
North Highfield FUL/RIB PR2 13
Northlands CROS/BRETH PR26 3
  FUL/RIB PR2 12
Northleach Av PRES PR1 28
North Meadowside
  KIRK/FR/WA PR4 28

Nor - Reg 57

h Ribble St *BER* PR5 ....19 E5
h Rd *PRES* PR1 ....3 F1
ES PR1 ....18 B2
nside *CHLY/EC* PR7 ....39 E4
n St *CHLYE* PR6 ....40 C5
ES PR1 ....2 E2
numberland St
LY/EC PR7 ....44 D3
h Union Vw
OS/BRETH PR26 ....31 F2
hway *FUL/RIB* PR2 ....11 H4
R/LONG PR3 ....6 C2
wich PR1 *PRES* PR1 ....3 H5
ingham Rd *PRES* PR1 ....18 C2
ery Cl *CHLY/EC* PR7 ....46 C1
YL PR25 ....35 F4
ery La *KIRK/FR/WA* PR4 ....29 C1
er Rd *PRES* PR1 ....2 C4

O

Av *CHLY/EC* PR7 ....39 F4
R/LONG PR3 ....15 B3
ES PR1 ....23 F3
Cft *CHLYE* PR6 ....37 F2
Dr *CHLYE* PR6 ....40 C4
engate *FUL/RIB* * PR1 ....13 E1
enhead St *PRES* * PR1 ....19 C2
ield *FUL/RIB* PR2 ....12 B1
L/RIB PR2 ....17 F2
ield Dr *CROS/BRETH* PR26 ......34 B3
Gv *KIRK/FR/WA* PR4 ....30 A3
ham Ct *PRES* PR1 ....3 H4
en and Gln *BER* PR5 ....24 C3
ands Dr *PRES* PR1 ....23 E2
ands Gv *FUL/RIB* PR2 ....16 D2
and St *BER* PR5 ....25 G5
mere *CHLYE* PR6 ....37 G1
idge Cl *FUL/RIB* PR2 ....12 B1
Oaks *BER* PR5 ....24 D3
LY/EC PR7 ....47 F1
shott Pl *BER* PR5 ....33 F2
St *PRES* PR1 ....3 H5
cree Av *FUL/RIB* PR2 ....11 E4
YL PR25 ....32 B5
cree Cl *FUL/RIB* PR2 ....11 E4
Vw *LEYL* PR25 ....35 F4
way *GAR/LONG* PR3 ....15 B2
wood Av *BER* PR5 ....25 C2
wood Dr *FUL/RIB* PR2 ....6 D5
wood Rd *CHLY/EC* PR7 ....44 B4
LY/EC PR7 ....46 D3
wood Vw *CHLY/EC* PR7 ....47 F1
worth Av *FUL/RIB* PR2 ....13 H3
n Ct *FUL/RIB* PR2 ....9 H4
n Crs *PRES* PR1 ....13 F5
Bridge Wy *CHLYE* PR6 ....44 D1
Cock Yd *PRES* PR1 ....3 G4
Cft *FUL/RIB* PR2 ....6 D5
ield *PRES* PR1 ....23 H4
ield Rd *BER* PR5 ....33 E2
Hall Cl *BER* PR5 ....32 C1
Hall Dr *BER* PR5 ....32 C1
Hey Cft *PRES* * PR1 ....23 H4
Lancaster La *FUL/RIB* PR2 ....17 H2
Lostock La *BER* PR5 ....32 C2
Mill Ct *KIRK/FR/WA* PR4 ....28 B5
Millstones *PRES* PR1 ....2 B5
Oak Gdns *PRES* PR1 ....24 C4
Orchard *FUL/RIB* PR2 ....11 H3
School Cl *CROS/BRETH* PR26 ...34 A4
School Dr *KIRK/FR/WA* PR4 .....28 D2
School La *BER* PR5 ....32 A3
LY/EC PR7 ....39 F4
Station Cl *FUL/RIB* PR2 ....9 H4
Tram Rd *PRES* PR1 ....24 C2
Vicarage *PRES* PR1 ....3 G3
e Cl *CHLYE* PR6 ....40 C2
er's Pl *FUL/RIB* PR2 ....7 C5
Orchard *KIRK/FR/WA* PR4 ....5 C3
hard Av *KIRK/FR/WA* PR4 ....30 A2
hard Cl *CHLY/EC* PR7 ....39 F3
JL/RIB PR2 ....11 E3
hard Cft *BER* PR5 ....31 C1
hard Dr *CHLYE* PR6 ....40 C2
hard La *KIRK/FR/WA* PR4 ....28 B2
hard St *LEYL* PR25 ....35 H3
RES PR1 ....3 F3
Rd *FUL/RIB* PR2 ....17 G1
skirk Rd *PRES* PR1 ....3 G3
ell Cl *LEYL* PR25 ....34 D3
est Rd *PRES* PR1 ....20 A2
ert Cft *KIRK/FR/WA* PR4 ....28 C1
orne Dr *CHLYE* PR6 ....37 G2
orne Rd *BER* PR5 ....25 F3
orne St *PRES* PR1 ....2 C5

P

Osprey Cl *CHLYE* PR6 ....41 G4
Oswald Rd *FUL/RIB* PR2 ....17 G2
Otters Cl *FUL/RIB* PR2 ....18 B2
Otway St *PRES* PR1 ....18 A1
Outram Wy *BER* PR5 ....32 C1
Overton Rd *FUL/RIB* PR2 ....16 C3
Owens Cl *CHLYE* * PR6 ....45 E3
Owen St *PRES* PR1 ....3 K2
Owtram St *PRES* PR1 ....19 G5
Oxford Rd *BER* PR5 ....32 D1
FUL/RIB PR2 ....11 H4
Oxford St *CHLY/EC* PR7 ....44 C4
PRES PR1 ....3 H5
Ox Hey Av *FUL/RIB* * PR2 ....16 A2
Oxheys St *PRES* PR1 ....17 H1
Oxley Gv *PRES* PR1 ....19 H2
Oxley Rd North *PRES* * PR1 .....19 F2
Oystons MI *FUL/RIB* * PR2 ....17 G3

The Paddock *FUL/RIB* PR2 ....12 C2
Paddock Av *CROS/BRETH* PR26 ...34 A4
Padway *PRES* PR1 ....23 H4
Pages Ct *BER* PR5 ....31 H2
Paley Rd *PRES* PR1 ....2 B4
Pall MI *CHLY/EC* PR7 ....44 C4
Paradise Cl *CHLYE* PR6 ....37 F4
Paradise La *CROS/BRETH* PR26 ...34 B3
Paradise St *CHLYE* PR6 ....41 F4
Park Av *CHLY/EC* PR7 ....39 F5
KIRK/FR/WA PR4 ....22 C5
PRES PR1 ....18 D1
Park Cl *PRES* PR1 ....23 H2
Park Dr *FUL/RIB* PR2 ....16 B2
Parker La *KIRK/FR/WA* PR4 ......30 C3
Parker St *CHLY/EC* PR7 ....44 C1
PRES PR1 ....17 H1
Park Farm Cl *KIRK/FR/WA* PR4 ...28 B2
Parkfield Av *FUL/RIB* PR2 ....17 F1
Parkfield Cl *FUL/RIB* PR2 ....16 A2
Parkfield Crs *FUL/RIB* PR2 ....16 A3
Parkgate Dr *LEYL* PR25 ....35 E5
Parklands Av *PRES* PR1 ....23 E2
Parklands Cl *PRES* PR1 ....23 E2
Parklands Dr *FUL/RIB* PR2 ....7 E5
Parklands Gv *FUL/RIB* PR2 ....7 E5
Park La *PRES* PR1 ....24 A3
Park Mill Pl *PRES* PR1 ....3 G1
Park Pl *BER* PR5 ....25 G2
PRES PR1 ....3 G5
Park Rd *CHLY/EC* PR7 ....44 C2
CHLY/EC PR7 ....46 C4
FUL/RIB PR2 ....12 C4
LEYL PR25 ....35 G5
PRES PR1 ....23 H2
Parkside *FUL/RIB* PR2 ....16 B1
PRES PR1 ....12 D5
Parkside Av *CHLY/EC* PR7 ....44 C4
Parkside Dr *CHLYE* PR6 ....40 B1
Parkside Dr South *CHLYE* PR6 ...40 B1
Park St *CHLY/EC* PR7 ....42 C4
CHLY/EC PR7 ....44 C2
Parkthorn Rd *FUL/RIB* PR2 ....16 A3
Park Vw *FUL/RIB* PR2 ....23 H2
Park View Av *FUL/RIB* * PR2 .....17 F1
Park Wy *PRES* PR1 ....23 H2
Parlick Av *GAR/LONG* PR3 ....15 C3
Parlick Rd *FUL/RIB* * PR2 ....20 A1
Parr Cottage Cl *CHLY/EC* PR7 ...42 C3
Parr La *CHLY/EC* PR7 ....42 B3
Parrock Cl *PRES* PR1 ....23 H2
Parson's Brow *CHLY/EC* PR7 ....44 C3
Pasture Field Cl
CROS/BRETH PR26 ....34 B4
The Pastures *FUL/RIB* PR2 ....9 H4
Pastures New *BER* PR5 ....32 A1
Patten St *PRES* PR1 ....2 E2
The Pavilions *FUL/RIB* PR2 ....17 G4
Peachtree Cl *FUL/RIB* PR2 ....13 F2
Peacock Hall Rd *LEYL* PR25 .....34 D5
Peacock Hill Cl *FUL/RIB* PR2 ....14 B1
Pearfield *LEYL* PR25 ....35 G2
Pear Tree Av *CHLY/EC* PR7 ......46 D2
Pear Tree Cl *BER* * PR5 ....25 G4
Pear Tree Crs *BER* PR5 ....25 G4
Pear Tree Cft *KIRK/FR/WA* PR4 ...28 C2
Pear Tree La *CHLY/EC* PR7 ....39 G4
Pear Tree Rd *CHLYE* PR6 ....37 F1
Pear Tree St *BER* * PR5 ....25 G4
Pechell St *PRES* PR1 ....17 G2
Pedders Gv *FUL/RIB* PR2 ....17 E3
Pedders La *FUL/RIB* PR2 ....17 E2
Pedder St *PRES* PR1 ....2 C2
Pedders Wy *FUL/RIB* PR2 ....17 E3
Peel Hall St *PRES* PR1 ....3 J1

Peel St *CHLY/EC* PR7 ....44 C3
PRES PR1 ....2 C2
Pembroke Pl *CHLY/EC* PR7 ......44 B4
LEYL PR25 ....35 G4
PRES * PR1 ....3 H4
Pembury Av *PRES* PR1 ....24 A3
Pendle Ct *GAR/LONG* PR3 ....15 B4
Pendle Hill Cl *FUL/RIB* PR2 ......14 C1
Pendle Rd *LEYL* PR25 ....36 B3
Penguin St *PRES* PR1 ....18 D2
Pennine Av *CHLY/EC* PR7 ....43 B1
Pennine Rd *CHLYE* PR6 ....45 C2
The Pennines *FUL/RIB* PR2 ......12 C1
Penny St *PRES* PR1 ....3 G2
Penwortham Ct *PRES* PR1 ....23 H2
Penwortham Hall Gdns
PRES PR1 ....24 A3
Penwortham Wy *PRES* PR1 ......23 F2
Percy St *CHLY/EC* PR7 ....44 D3
PRES PR1 ....3 H3
Peregrine Pl *CROS/BRETH* PR26 ...34 D2
Peterfield Rd *PRES* * PR1 ....24 A4
Peter St *CHLY/EC* PR7 ....44 C4
Petunia Cl *LEYL* PR25 ....36 C2
The Pickerings *BER* * PR5 ....32 A1
Pilling Cl *CHLY/EC* PR7 ....44 D4
Pilling La *CHLY/EC* PR7 ....43 H2
Pincock Brow *CHLY/EC* PR7 .....43 A2
Pincock St *CHLY/EC* PR7 ....43 A2
Pine Cl *FUL/RIB* * PR2 ....13 H4
Pine Gv *CHLYE* PR6 ....40 D4
Pines Cl *BER* PR5 ....33 G5
Pine Wks *FUL/RIB* PR2 ....16 A2
Pineway *FUL/RIB* PR2 ....11 G4
Pinewood Av *GAR/LONG* PR3 ...6 C2
Pinewood Crs *LEYL* PR25 ....35 E4
Pinfold *KIRK/FR/WA* PR4 ....28 C2
Pinfold St *PRES* PR1 ....19 F3
Pingle Cft *CHLYE* PR6 ....37 E2
Pittman Ct *FUL/RIB* PR2 ....12 D1
Pittman Wy *FUL/RIB* PR2 ....7 H5
Pitt St *PRES* PR1 ....2 D4
Plant St *FUL/RIB* * PR2 ....17 G2
Pleasant Vw *CHLY/EC* PR7 ....46 D3
Plevna Rd *PRES* PR1 ....19 E3
The Ploughlands *FUL/RIB* PR2 ...16 C2
Plover St *PRES* PR1 ....18 D1
Plumpton Fld *KIRK/FR/WA* PR4 ...5 G3
Plumpton Rd *FUL/RIB* PR2 ....17 C1
Plumtree Cl *FUL/RIB* PR2 ....13 E2
Plungington Rd *FUL/RIB* PR2 ....12 A5
PRES PR1 ....18 A1
Plymouth Gv *CHLYE* PR6 ....45 E2
Polefield *FUL/RIB* PR2 ....12 A1
Pole St *PRES* PR1 ....3 H3
Pollard St *PRES* PR1 ....2 D2
Poole Rd *FUL/RIB* PR2 ....12 C4
Pool House La *FUL/RIB* PR2 .....10 D3
Pope La *FUL/RIB* PR2 ....14 A5
FUL/RIB PR2 ....19 H1
KIRK/FR/WA PR4 ....23 H5
PRES PR1 ....23 H3
Pope Wk *PRES* PR1 ....23 H3
Poplar Av *BER* PR5 ....25 H5
CHLY/EC PR7 ....39 E3
KIRK/FR/WA PR4 ....28 D2
Poplar Cl *BER* PR5 ....25 H5
Poplar Dr *GAR/LONG* PR3 ....15 B2
PRES PR1 ....23 G1
Poplar Gv *BER* PR5 ....25 H5
FUL/RIB PR2 ....14 A4
Poplar St *CHLY/EC* PR7 ....44 D4
Poppy Av *CHLYE* PR6 ....40 D5
Poppyfield *KIRK/FR/WA* PR4 ....10 D2
Porter Pl *PRES* PR1 ....3 G6
Porter St *PRES* PR1 ....18 D2
Portland St *CHLY/EC* PR7 ....44 D2
PRES PR1 ....2 B5
Portman St *PRES* PR1 ....19 E1
Portree Cl *PRES* PR1 ....13 E3
Portsmouth Dr *CHLYE* PR6 ....45 E2
Port Wy *PRES* PR1 ....2 A5
Potter La *BER* PR5 ....25 H5
Poulton Crs *BER* PR5 ....26 D3
Poulton St *FUL/RIB* PR2 ....17 G2
Powis Rd *FUL/RIB* PR2 ....17 E3
Poynter St *PRES* PR1 ....19 E2
Preesall Rd *FUL/RIB* PR2 ....16 C2
Preston New Rd *BER* PR5 ....20 B3
BER PR5 ....21 H2
Preston Nook *CHLY/EC* PR7 .....42 C5
Preston Rd *BER* PR5 ....33 F4
CHLY/EC PR7 ....46 A1
CHLYE PR6 ....37 F1
CHLYE PR6 ....40 B1
FUL/RIB PR2 ....9 H4
GAR/LONG PR3 ....15 B4
LEYL PR25 ....35 H2

Preston St *CHLYE* PR6 ....40 C5
Primrose Gv *PRES* PR1 ....13 E5
Primrose Hl *PRES* PR1 ....3 K4
Primrose Hill Rd *CHLY/EC* PR7 ...38 D3
Primrose La *PRES* PR1 ....13 E5
Primrose Rd *PRES* PR1 ....13 E5
Primrose St *CHLYE* PR6 ....44 D2
Princes Ct *PRES* PR1 ....17 F5
Princes Dr *FUL/RIB* PR2 ....11 H2
Prince's Rd *BER* PR5 ....25 G1
PRES PR1 ....17 F5
Princess St *BER* PR5 ....31 H2
BER PR5 ....32 D1
CHLY/EC PR7 ....44 D4
LEYL PR25 ....35 H3
PRES PR1 ....3 J5
Princess Wy *CHLY/EC* PR7 ....39 F5
Pringle Wd *GAR/LONG* PR3 .....6 C3
Priory Cl *LEYL* PR25 ....36 A2
PRES PR1 ....17 G5
Priory Crs *PRES* PR1 ....17 G5
Priory La *PRES* PR1 ....17 G5
Priory St *FUL/RIB* PR2 ....2 B2
Progress St *CHLYE* PR6 ....45 E2
Prospect Av *BER* PR5 ....31 H1
Prospect Ct *GAR/LONG* PR3 ....15 C4
Prospect Pl *FUL/RIB* PR2 ....17 F2
PRES PR1 ....24 A2
Pudding Pie Nook La
GAR/LONG PR3 ....7 F1
Pump St *PRES* PR1 ....3 H2

Q

Quaker Brook La *BER* PR5 ....27 G3
Quarry Rd *CHLYE* PR6 ....45 E4
Queenscourt Av *PRES* PR1 ....24 A4
Queensdale Cl *BER* PR5 ....25 G2
Queens Dr *FUL/RIB* PR2 ....11 H2
GAR/LONG PR3 ....15 A3
Queensgate *CHLY/EC* PR7 ....44 B3
Queen's Gv *CHLY/EC* PR7 ....44 C2
Queen's Rd *BER* PR5 ....25 G2
CHLY/EC PR7 ....44 B2
FUL/RIB * PR2 ....11 H5
Queen St *BER* PR5 ....31 H2
PRES PR1 ....3 J4
Queen St East *CHLY/EC* PR7 ....44 D4
Queensway *BER* PR5 ....25 G5
CHLY/EC PR7 ....39 G5
FUL/RIB PR2 ....16 D1
LEYL PR25 ....35 E5
PRES PR1 ....17 F5
Queensway Cl *PRES* PR1 ....17 F5
Quin St *LEYL* PR25 ....35 G3

R

Radburn Brow *CHLYE* PR6 ....37 F1
Radburn Cl *CHLYE* PR6 ....37 F1
Radnor St *PRES* PR1 ....2 D2
Raglan St *FUL/RIB* PR2 ....17 H1
Raikes Rd *PRES* PR1 ....19 E2
Railway Rd *CHLYE* PR6 ....44 D1
Railway St *CHLY/EC* PR7 ....44 D3
LEYL PR25 ....35 H2
Raleigh Rd *FUL/RIB* PR2 ....12 A2
Ramsey Av *PRES* PR1 ....13 F5
Ranaldsway *LEYL* PR25 ....34 C4
Ranglet Rd *BER* PR5 ....33 F2
Rangletts Av *CHLY/EC* PR7 ....44 C4
Ranglit Av *FUL/RIB* PR2 ....16 A2
Ratten La *KIRK/FR/WA* PR4 ......22 A3
Ravenhill Dr *CHLY/EC* PR7 ....44 C1
Raven St *PRES* PR1 ....19 E1
Ravenswood *FUL/RIB* PR2 ....19 G1
Rawcliffe Dr *FUL/RIB* PR2 ....16 C3
Rawcliffe Rd *CHLY/EC* PR7 ....44 C3
Rawstorne Rd *PRES* PR1 ....23 F1
Rectory Cl *CHLY/EC* PR7 ....44 C1
Redcar Av *FUL/RIB* PR2 ....10 D4
Red Cross St *PRES* PR1 ....2 C4
Redhill *KIRK/FR/WA* PR4 ....22 A5
Redhill Gv *CHLYE* PR6 ....41 E4
Red House La *CHLY/EC* PR7 .....42 B4
Redmayne St *PRES* PR1 ....19 F3
Redsands Dr *FUL/RIB* PR2 ....16 A2
Redwood Av *LEYL* PR25 ....35 E4
Redwood Dr *CHLY/EC* PR7 ....45 E4
GAR/LONG PR3 ....15 B2
Reedfield *BER* PR5 ....33 G5
Reedfield Pl *BER* PR5 ....32 D2
Reeveswood *CHLY/EC* PR7 ....42 B4
Regency Av *BER* PR5 ....32 B1

Regent Ct FUL/RIB PR2 ....12 A3
Regent Dr FUL/RIB PR2 ....11 H4
Regent Gv FUL/RIB PR2 ....12 A3
Regent Pk FUL/RIB PR2 ....12 A2
Regent Rd PR5 ....25 F2
  CHLY/EC PR7 ....44 B3
  LEYL * PR25 ....35 F3
Regent St CHLY/EC PR7 ....46 C4
  GAR/LONG PR3 ....15 A3
  PRES PR1 ....3 F6
Regentsway BER PR5 ....32 C1
Regents Wy CHLY/EC PR7 ....39 F5
Reigate CHLYE PR6 ....41 F4
Reiver Rd CROS/BRETH PR26 ......34 C1
Renshaw Dr BER PR5 ....3 G4
Rhoden Rd CROS/BRETH PR26 ....34 C3
Rhodesway BER PR5 ....27 E4
Ribble Bank PRES PR1 ....17 F5
Ribble Bank St PRES PR1 ....2 C4
Ribble Cl PRES PR1 ....24 A2
Ribble Ct FUL/RIB * PR2 ....17 G2
  PRES PR1 ....2 B6
Ribble Crs BER * PR5 ....19 E5
Ribble Rd LEYL PR25 ....34 D4
Ribblesdale Dr FUL/RIB PR2...........9 G5
Ribblesdale Pl CHLY/EC PR7..........44 B3
  PRES PR1 ....3 F6
Ribble St PRES PR1 ....2 C4
  FUL/RIB PR2 ....19 F1
Ribbleton Av FUL/RIB PR2 ....13 C5
  FUL/RIB PR2 ....19 F1
Ribbleton Hall Dr FUL/RIB PR2 ....13 H5
Ribbleton La PRES PR1 ....19 E2
Ribbleton Pl PRES PR1 ....3 K2
Ribbleton St PRES PR1 ....3 J2
Ribble Wy BER PR5 ....20 C1
Ribby Pl FUL/RIB PR2 ....16 D2
Richmond Ct CHLY/EC PR7 ....44 C4
  CROS/BRETH PR26 ....34 B3
Richmond Rd CHLY/EC PR7 ....42 C3
  CHLYE PR6 ....45 E4
Richmond St PRES PR1...................3 K4
Ridge Ct GAR/LONG PR3 ....15 D2
Ridgeford Gdns FUL/RIB PR2 ....11 H3
Ridgemont FUL/RIB PR2 ....11 G2
Ridge Rd CHLYE PR6 ....45 E3
Ridge Wy PRES PR1 ....24 A2
The Ridings CHLYE PR6 ....40 C1
Riding St PRES * PR1 ....3 F1
Ridley Rd FUL/RIB PR2 ....17 C1
Rigby St PRES PR1 ....19 E2
Rigby Wk CHLY/EC * PR7 ....44 C2
Ringway CHLY/EC PR7 ....44 A3
Ring Wy PRES PR1 ....3 H2
Ringwood Rd PRES PR1 ....19 E1
Ripon St PRES PR1 ....18 A1
Ripon Ter PRES PR1 ....19 H2
Risedale Dr GAR/LONG PR3 ....15 C3
River Hts BER PR5 ....32 A1
River Pde PRES PR1 ....2 B7
Riversedge Rd LEYL PR25.............34 C4
Riverside PRES PR1 ....32 C2
  PRES PR1 ....24 A1
Riverside Av CROS/BRETH PR26 ...31 E5
Riverside Cl CROS/BRETH PR26 ....31 E5
Riverside Rd PRES PR1 ....24 A1
River St PRES PR1 ....2 C4
Riversway FUL/RIB PR2 ....16 A3
  FUL/RIB PR2 ....16 D3
Riverway ST BER PR5 ....32 A1
Rivington Rd CHLYE PR6 ....45 E1
Roach Rd BER PR5........................21 E4
  BER PR5 ....27 H2
Roberts St CHLY/EC PR7 ....44 C3
Robin Cl CHLY/EC PR7 ....46 B2
Robin Hey CROS/BRETH PR26 .....34 B3
Robinson St FUL/RIB PR2.............11 H5
Robin St PRES PR1.......................19 F2
Rockburgh Crs KIRK/FR/WA PR4 ...28 C5
Rock Villa Rd CHLYE * PR6 ....37 G4
Rodney St PRES PR1 ....2 E2
Roebuck St CHLY/EC PR7 ....17 G1
Roe Hey Dr CHLY/EC PR7 ....46 D3
Roman Rd PRES PR1 ....3 K5
Roman Wy FUL/RIB PR2 ....14 C2
Romford Rd PRES PR1 ....19 E1
Ronaldsway PRES PR1 ....13 F5
Rookery Cl CHLY/EC PR7 ....44 A4
  PRES PR1 ....24 A4
Rookery Dr PRES PR1 ....24 B4
Rook St PRES PR1 ....18 D1
Rookwood CHLY/EC PR7 ....42 B4
Rookwood Av CHLY/EC PR7 ....40 C5
Roots La KIRK/FR/WA PR4 ....4 A2
Roseacre Pl FUL/RIB PR2 ....16 C2
Rose Av FUL/RIB PR2 ....11 G5
Rosebank FUL/RIB PR2.................16 A4
Roseberry Av KIRK/FR/WA PR4 ....10 C3
Rose Cl LEYL PR25 ....36 C2

Rosedene Cl KIRK/FR/WA PR4 .....10 C3
Rose Fold PRES PR1 ....23 H2
Rose La PRES PR1 ....13 E5
Rose Lea FUL/RIB PR2 ....13 F2
Rosemary Ct PRES PR1 ....23 G4
Rosemary La KIRK/FR/WA PR4 ......4 C3
Rosemeade Av BER PR5 ....31 H1
Rose St LEYL PR25 ....35 H1
  PRES PR1 ....3 H4
Rose Ter FUL/RIB PR2 ....17 F2
Roseway FUL/RIB PR2 ....17 E2
Rosewood KIRK/FR/WA PR4 ....10 C3
Rosewood Av BER PR5 ....26 C3
Rosewood Dr BER PR5 ....26 B3
Roshaw FUL/RIB PR2 ....9 G4
Rosklyn Rd CHLYE PR6 ....45 E3
Rossall Cl BER PR5 ....27 E2
Rossall Dr FUL/RIB PR2 ....11 G4
Rossall Rd CHLYE PR6 ....45 E1
  FUL/RIB PR2 ....11 G4
Rossall St FUL/RIB PR2 ....17 G2
Rostrevor Cl CROS/BRETH PR26 ...34 B3
Rotherwick Av CHLY/EC PR7 ....44 B3
Rothwell Ct LEYL PR25 ....35 G2
Rothwell Crs FUL/RIB PR2 ....13 H4
Rough Hey FUL/RIB PR2 ....14 B1
Rough Hey Rd FUL/RIB PR2 ....14 B1
Round Acre BER PR5.....................24 C5
Round Meadow FUL/RIB PR2 ....9 H4
  CROS/BRETH PR26 ....34 C3
Roundway Down FUL/RIB PR2 .....11 G1
Round Wd PRES PR1 ....17 F4
Rowan Av FUL/RIB PR2 ....14 A4
Rowan Cl PRES PR1 ....23 F3
Rowan Cft CHLYE PR6 ....37 F5
Rowangate FUL/RIB PR2 ....13 E1
Rowan Gv CHLYE PR6 ....40 C4
Rowberrow Cl FUL/RIB PR2 ....13 F2
Roworth Cl BER PR5 ....25 G3
Rowton Heath FUL/RIB PR2 ....11 G1
Royal Av FUL/RIB PR2 ....12 A2
  LEYL PR25 ....35 E5
Royalty Av KIRK/FR/WA PR4 ....30 A1
Royalty Gdns KIRK/FR/WA PR4 ...30 A1
Royalty La KIRK/FR/WA PR4 ....30 A1
Royle Cl CHLY/EC PR7 ....44 B2
Royton Dr CHLYE PR6 ....40 C2
Rufus St PRES PR1 ....19 E1
Rundle Rd FUL/RIB PR2 ....11 H5
Runshaw Hall La CHLY/EC PR7 ....38 C3
Runshaw La CHLY/EC PR7 ....38 A4
  CHLY/EC PR7 ....39 E4
Rushy Hey BER PR5......................31 G1
Ruskin Av LEYL PR25 ....35 G2
Ruskin St PRES PR1........................3 K6
Rusland Dr BER PR5 ....27 E2
Russell Av LEYL PR25 ....36 A4
  PRES PR1 ....20 A3
Russell Sq CHLYE PR6 ....44 D1
Russell Sq West CHLYE PR6 ....44 D1
Rutland Av BER * PR5 ....25 F3
Rutland St PRES PR1 ....19 E3
Rydal Av BER PR5 ....25 F5
  PRES PR1 ....23 G3
Rydal Cl FUL/RIB PR2 ....13 E4
Rydal Pl CHLY/EC PR7 ....44 C4
Rydal Rd PRES PR1 ....19 F1
Ryddingwood PRES PR1 ....17 F5
Ryden Av LEYL PR25 ....36 A3
Ryding Cl CROS/BRETH PR26 ......35 E1
Ryefield CHLYE PR6 ....41 G1
Ryefield Av PRES PR1 ....23 H4
Ryelands Crs FUL/RIB PR2 ....16 C3
Rye St PRES PR1 ....18 C2
Rylands Rd CHLY/EC PR7 ....44 B3

S

Sackville St CHLYE PR6 ....45 E3
Sagar St CHLY/EC PR7 ....42 C4
Sage Ct PRES PR1 ....23 G4
Sage La PRES PR1 ....12 D5
St Aidans Pk BER PR5 ....25 G4
St Alban's Pl CHLY/EC PR7 ....44 D5
St Ambrose Ter PRES * LEYL PR25 ...35 H2
St Andrew's Av FUL/RIB PR2 ....17 E1
St Andrews Cl CHLYE PR6 ....39 F3
  LEYL PR25 ....35 G4
St Andrew's Rd PRES * PR1 ....18 C1
St Andrews Wy LEYL PR25 ....35 G4
Saint Annes Rd CHLYE PR6 ....45 E3
St Anne's Rd LEYL PR25 ....36 A2
St Anne's St PRES PR1 ....18 C1
St Anthony's Cl FUL/RIB * PR2 .....11 G4
St Anthony's Crs FUL/RIB PR2 ......11 G4
St Anthony's Dr FUL/RIB PR2 ....11 G4

St Anthony's Rd PRES * PR1 ....18 C1
St Austin's Pl PRES PR1 ....3 H5
St Austin's Rd PRES PR1 ....3 H5
St Barnabas' Pl PRES PR1 ....3 H1
St Catherines Cl LEYL PR25 ....36 A2
St Catherine's Dr FUL/RIB PR2 .....11 G4
St Catherines Wy BER PR5............32 A2
St Chad's Rd PRES PR1 ....19 E2
St Christines Av LEYL PR25 ....32 A5
St Christopher's Rd PRES * PR1 ....18 C1
St Clares Av FUL/RIB PR2 ....12 C2
St Clements Av LEYL PR25 ....36 A1
St Cuthbert's Cl FUL/RIB PR2 ......11 H5
St Cuthbert's Rd BER PR5 ....24 C5
  PRES * PR1 ....18 C1
St David's Rd LEYL PR25 ....36 A2
  PRES * PR1 ....18 C1
St Francis Cl FUL/RIB PR2 ....12 C1
St George's Rd PRES PR1 ....18 B1
St George's St CHLY/EC PR7.........44 C3
St Gerrard's Rd BER PR5 ....24 C5
St Gregory Rd PRES PR1 ....18 D1
St Gregory's Pl CHLY/EC PR7 ....44 C5
St Helen's Rd CHLYE PR6 ....37 G3
St Hilda's Cl CHLY/EC PR7 ....47 C1
St Ignatius' Sq PRES PR1 ....3 G2
St Ives Crs FUL/RIB PR2 ....11 E4
St James Cl BER PR5....................31 H1
St James's Gdns
  CROS/BRETH PR26 ....34 A4
St James's Pl CHLYE PR6..............45 E3
St James's Rd PRES PR1 ....18 B1
St Johns Cl CHLYE PR6 ....37 F5
St John's Gn LEYL PR25................35 E3
St John's Pl PRES PR1 ....3 G4
St John's Rd BER PR5 ....25 F1
St Josephs Pl CHLYE PR6 ....44 D1
St Joseph's Ter PRES * PR1 ....19 E2
St Jude's Av BER PR5 ....25 F5
  LEYL PR25 ....32 A5
St Luke's Pl PRES PR1 ....19 E2
St Margarets Cl FUL/RIB PR2 ....11 E4
St Margaret's Rd LEYL PR25 ....36 A2
St Mark's Pl East PRES * PR1..........2 A2
St Mark's Pl West PRES * PR1 ....2 A2
St Mark's Rd PRES PR1 ....2 A2
St Marlow Av LEYL * PR25 ....36 A1
St Martin's Rd PRES * PR1 ....18 C1
St Mary's Av BER PR5 ....25 F5
St Mary's Cl BER PR5 ....25 F5
  GAR/LONG * PR3 ....15 B2
  PRES * PR1 ....19 E3
St Mary's Ct PRES PR1 ....3 K3
St Mary's Ga CHLY/EC PR7 ....39 E4
St Mary's Rd BER PR5 ....25 G5
St Mary's St PRES PR1 ....3 K2
St Mary's St North PRES PR1..........3 J2
St Michael's Cl CHLY/EC PR7 ....44 B1
  FUL/RIB PR2 ....11 H5
St Michael's Rd LEYL * PR25.........36 A1
  PRES * PR1 ....18 C1
St Oswalds Cl PRES PR1 ....19 E1
St Paul's Av PRES PR1 ....3 G1
St Pauls Cl CROS/BRETH PR26 ....31 F2
St Paul's Rd PRES PR1 ....18 C1
St Paul's Sq PRES PR1 ....3 H2
St Peters Cl PRES PR1 ....2 E2
St Peter's Sq PRES PR1 ....2 D2
St Peter's St CHLYE PR6 ....45 E1
  PRES PR1 ....2 E2
St Philip's Rd PRES * PR1 ....18 C1
St Saviour's Cl BER PR5 ....32 D1
St Stephen's Rd PRES PR1............18 C1
St Theresa's Dr FUL/RIB PR2 ....11 G4
St Thomas' Pl PRES * PR1..............2 E1
St Thomas St PRES PR1................18 B1
St Thomas's Rd CHLY/EC PR7 ......44 C2
St Thomas' St PRES PR1 ....18 B1
St Vincents Rd FUL/RIB PR2 ....12 A3
St Walburge Av PRES PR1...............2 C2
St Walburges Gdns FUL/RIB PR2....2 B2
St Wilfrid's Ter GAR/LONG PR3 ...15 B3
St Wilfrid St PRES PR1....................2 E1
Salisbury Rd PRES PR1 ....2 B5
Salisbury St CHLY/EC * PR7..........44 D3
  PRES PR1 ....19 F2
Salmon St PRES PR1.....................19 E4
Salter St PRES PR1.......................18 D1
Salwick Pl FUL/RIB PR2 ....16 C2
Samuel St PRES PR1 ....19 F3
Sandfield St LEYL PR25 ....35 H3
Sandgate CHLY/EC PR7 ....44 D5
Sandham St CHLYE PR6................44 D2
Sandridge Av CHLY/EC PR7 ....44 B3
Sandringham Av LEYL PR25 ....36 A3
Sandringham Park Dr
  KIRK/FR/WA PR4 ....29 D1
Sandringham Rd BER PR5 ....25 F3

  CHLY/EC PR7 1
Sandringham Wy
  KIRK/FR/WA PR4.......................1
Sandsdale Av FUL/RIB PR2...........1
Sandwick Cl FUL/RIB PR2.............1
Sandybrook Cl FUL/RIB PR2.........1
Sandycroft FUL/RIB PR2................1
Sandyfields KIRK/FR/WA PR4........1
Sandyforth La KIRK/FR/WA PR4 1
Sandygate La GAR/LONG PR3.......1
Sandy La CHLYE PR6.....................1
  KIRK/FR/WA PR4........................1
  LEYL PR25..................................1
Sandy Pl LEYL PR25......................1
Saul St PRES PR1...........................1
Saunders' La KIRK/FR/WA PR4......2
  KIRK/FR/WA PR4........................1
Saunders Ms CHLY/EC PR7...........4
Savick Av FUL/RIB PR2..................1
Savick Ct BER PR5.........................1
Savick Rd FUL/RIB PR2.................1
Savick Wy FUL/RIB PR2.................1
Saville St CHLY/EC PR7..................4
Savoy St PRES PR1.........................1
Sawley Crs FUL/RIB PR2...............1
Saxon Hey FUL/RIB PR2................1
Scarlet St CHLYE PR6.....................1
Scarlett Dr KIRK/FR/WA PR4.........2
Scawfell Rd CHLY/EC PR7.............1
Sceptre Wy BER PR5......................3
Schleswig St PRES PR1...................1
Schleswig Wy LEYL PR25...............3
Scholars Gn FUL/RIB PR2..............1
School Brow CHLYE PR6................3
School Fld BER PR5.......................1
School La BER PR5.........................1
  BER PR5.....................................1
  CHLY/EC PR7.............................4
  CROS/BRETH PR26....................3
  KIRK/FR/WA PR4........................4
  KIRK/FR/WA PR4........................4
  LEYL PR25..................................3
School St BER PR5.........................3
  KIRK/FR/WA PR4........................4
  LEYL PR25..................................3
  PRES PR1...................................1
Scotforth Rd PRES PR1..................1
Scott's Wd FUL/RIB PR2................1
Sea Vw KIRK/FR/WA PR4...............4
Sedberg St FUL/RIB PR2................1
Sedgefield KIRK/FR/WA PR4...........2
Sedgwick St PRES PR1...................1
Seedlee Rd PRES PR1....................3
Seed St PRES PR1..........................1
Sefton Rd BER PR5........................3
Selborne St PRES PR1....................1
Selby St PRES PR1.........................1
Selkirk Dr BER PR5.........................1
Sellers St PRES PR1........................1
Sephton St BER PR5.......................3
Sergeant St BER PR5......................3
Seven Acres BER PR5.....................3
Sevenoaks CHLY/EC PR7...............4
Seven Sands KIRK/FR/WA PR4.......2
Seven Stars Rd
  CROS/BRETH PR26....................3
  LEYL PR25..................................3
Severn Dr BER PR5........................3
Severn HI FUL/RIB PR2..................3
Severn St GAR/LONG PR3.............1
Seymour Ct PRES PR1...................1
Seymour Rd FUL/RIB PR2.............3
Seymour St CHLYE PR6.................4
Shady La BER PR5..........................3
Shaftesbury Av
  KIRK/FR/WA PR4........................2
  PRES PR1...................................1
Shaftesbury Pl CHLY/EC PR7.........4
Shakespeare Rd PRES PR1............1
Shakespeare Ter CHLYE PR6.........3
Shalgrove Fld FUL/RIB PR2............1
Sharoe Green La FUL/RIB PR2.......1
Sharoe Green Pk FUL/RIB PR2.......1
Sharoe Mount Av FUL/RIB PR2......1
Sharratts Pth CHLY/EC PR7...........4
Shawbrook Cl CHLY/EC PR7..........3
Shaw Brook Rd LEYL PR25............3
Shaw Brow CHLYE PR6..................3
Shaw HI CHLYE PR6........................4
Shaw Hill Dr CHLYE PR6................4
Shaw Hill St CHLY/EC PR7.............4
Shaw St PRES PR1.........................1
Shaw La GAR/LONG PR3...............1
Sheep Hill Brow CHLYE PR6...........3
Sheep Hill La CHLYE PR6...............3
Sheephill La KIRK/FR/WA PR4........2
Sheffield Dr FUL/RIB PR2..............1
Sheldon Ct PRES * PR1..................1

...y Cl CHLY/EC PR7 .....46 D5
...y Dr CHLY/EC PR7 .....42 D5
...y Ms FUL/RIB PR2 .....17 G2
...y Rd FUL/RIB PR2 .....17 G1
...v Road MI FUL/RIB * PR2 .....17 G2
...herd St PRES PR1 .....3 H4
...herds Wy CHLY/EC PR7 .....44 D2
...ton Pk FUL/RIB PR2 .....11 E2
...ourne Crs PRES PR1 .....12 C5
...ourne St CHLYE PR6 .....44 D3
...urn Rd PRES PR1 .....24 A3
...lley Rd BER PR5 .....31 H2
...wood Pl CHLYE PR6 .....44 D2
...wood Wy FUL/RIB PR2 .....12 C2
...Bank Crs FUL/RIB PR2 .....12 A2
...y La KIRK/FR/WA PR4 .....28 C1
...La BER PR5 .....26 B2
...eworth Rd PRES PR1 .....18 B1
...ling Fields La BER PR5 .....26 C3
...ring Brow Preston Rd
   .Y/EC PR7 .....46 C4
   L PR25 .....38 D1
...dale Cl BER PR5 .....27 E2
   L PR25 .....38 D1
...dale Dr FUL/RIB PR2 .....13 F3
...dale Rd CHLYE PR6 .....45 E3
...St PRES PR1 .....3 H6
...ster Rd FUL/RIB PR2 .....16 C1
...ons Av BER PR5 .....24 D3
...ton St PRES * PR1 .....2 E5
...eton FUL/RIB PR2 .....12 B1
...eton Cl FUL/RIB PR2 .....12 B1
...eton Rw PRES PR1 .....2 E2
...Cl FUL/RIB PR2 .....13 H4
...cre La KIRK/FR/WA PR4 .....29 A3
...ouse St PRES PR1 .....2 D3
...St PRES PR1 .....18 B2
...ington Rd PRES PR1 .....18 D1
...on Cl BER PR5 .....25 G4
...on Crs FUL/RIB PR2 .....13 G3
...St PRES PR1 .....2 C4
...urn Pl PRES PR1 .....20 A1
...urn Rd FUL/RIB PR2 .....19 H1
...r La LEYL PR25 .....34 D2
...ey Cft PRES PR1 .....24 B3
...m's Cl BER PR5 .....25 H4
...ay Cl PRES PR1 .....24 A3
...erset Av CHLY/EC PR7 .....44 C1
...erset Pk FUL/RIB PR2 .....11 F1
...erset Rd LEYL PR25 .....35 H2
...ES PR1 .....18 C2
...el Ct PRES PR1 .....23 G4
...h Av CHLY/EC PR7 .....44 D4
...K/FR/WA PR4 .....29 D1
   .....F5
...hbrook Rd LEYL PR25 .....35 E3
...h Cliff St PRES PR1 .....2 B6
...ndowns Rd CHLY/EC PR7 .....44 D5
...h Dr FUL/RIB PR2 .....7 E5
...h End PRES PR1 .....24 A1
...hern Av PRES PR1 .....3 K6
...hern Cl GAR/LONG PR3 .....15 B4
...hern Pde PRES PR1 .....3 K6
...hey Cl FUL/RIB PR2 .....12 B1
...hfield Dr KIRK/FR/WA PR4 .....29 D2
...ngate FUL/RIB PR2 .....11 H3
...ES PR1 .....18 B2
...hgates CHLY/EC PR7 .....46 B5
...n Gv FUL/RIB PR2 .....7 E5
...hlands Av BER PR5 .....24 D5
...hlands Dr
   OS/BRETH PR26 .....34 C5
...h Meadow La PRES PR1 .....2 C1
...h Meadow St PRES * PR1 .....3 H2
...ES * PR1 .....3 J3
...nport Rd CHLY/EC PR7 .....44 A2
...nport Ter CHLYE PR6 .....45 E4
...h Ribble St BER PR5 .....19 E5
...h Rd CHLYE PR6 .....46 C4
...nside CHLY/EC PR7 .....39 E4
...h Vw Ter LEYL PR25 .....35 G4
...Rd PRES PR1 .....2 B3
   .....A2
...dmore La CHLY/EC PR7 .....46 B5
...Cl LEYL PR25 .....35 E4
...ners Sq BER * PR5 .....32 C2
...spinney CHLYE PR6 .....40 C5
...PR1 .....22 D3

Spinney Brow FUL/RIB PR2 .....13 F4
Spinney Cl CHLYE PR6 .....40 B1
   KIRK/FR/WA PR4 .....29 D1
Spires Gv KIRK/FR/WA PR4 .....10 C3
Spring Bank PRES PR1 .....2 C5
Spring Crs CHLYE PR6 .....41 E1
Springcroft LEYL PR25 .....36 A1
Springfield Rd CHLY/EC * PR7 .....44 C2
   CHLY/EC PR7 .....44 C2
   LEYL PR25 .....34 D5
Springfield Rd North
   CHLY/EC * PR7 .....46 C4
Springfield St PRES PR1 .....18 A2
Spring Gdns LEYL PR25 .....35 F4
   PRES PR1 .....24 B4
Spring Meadow LEYL PR25 .....36 C2
Spring Ms CHLYE PR6 .....41 E1
Springsands Cl FUL/RIB * PR2 .....13 C3
Springs Rd CHLYE PR6 .....40 D5
   GAR/LONG PR3 .....15 C2
Spring St LEYL PR25 .....35 H3
Springwood Cl BER PR5 .....24 C3
Springwood Cottages
   CHLYE * PR6 .....45 E5
Springwood Dr CHLYE PR6 .....45 E5
Spruce Cl FUL/RIB PR2 .....13 E1
The Square LEYL PR25 .....35 H3
Squares Ct BER PR5 .....27 E4
Squire's Gate Rd FUL/RIB PR2 .....11 G5
Squires Rd PRES PR1 .....24 A4
Squires Wd FUL/RIB PR2 .....13 F2
Squirrel Fold FUL/RIB PR2 .....19 H1
Squirrel's Cha BER PR5 .....31 G2
Stack Cft CHLYE PR6 .....37 E2
Stafford Rd PRES PR1 .....18 C2
Staining Av FUL/RIB PR2 .....16 D3
Stamford Dr CHLYE PR6 .....40 C2
Standish St CHLY/EC PR7 .....44 C3
Stanhope St PRES PR1 .....17 H1
Stanifield Cl LEYL PR25 .....35 H1
Stanifield La BER PR5 .....35 H2
   LEYL PR25 .....35 H2
Stanley Av KIRK/FR/WA PR4 .....29 A5
   LEYL PR25 .....32 A5
   PRES PR1 .....24 A1
Stanley Cl GAR/LONG PR3 .....15 C3
Stanley Cft KIRK/FR/WA PR4 .....6 B2
Stanleyfield Cl PRES PR1 .....3 H1
Stanleyfield Rd PRES PR1 .....3 H1
Stanley Fold PRES PR1 .....31 F1
Stanley Gv PRES PR1 .....23 E2
Stanley Pl CHLY/EC PR7 .....44 C2
   PRES PR1 .....2 A5
Stanley Rd LEYL PR25 .....32 A5
Stanley St GAR/LONG * PR3 .....15 C3
   LEYL PR25 .....35 H3
   PRES PR1 .....3 J3
Stanley Ter PRES PR1 .....2 C5
Stanning Cl LEYL PR25 .....35 E4
Stansford Ct PRES PR1 .....23 H2
Stansted Rd CHLY/EC PR7 .....44 A3
Starkie St LEYL PR25 .....35 H3
   PRES PR1 .....3 F5
Starrgate Dr FUL/RIB PR2 .....16 C2
Startley Nook FUL/RIB PR4 .....30 B3
Station Rd BER PR5 .....27 H4
   BER PR5 .....27 H4
   CHLYE PR6 .....41 E1
   CHLY/EC PR7 .....46 D4
   PRES PR1 .....29 D1
Staveley Pl FUL/RIB PR2 .....16 C1
Steeley La CHLYE PR6 .....44 D3
Steeple Vw FUL/RIB PR2 .....2 A2
Stefano Rd PRES PR1 .....19 E3
Stephendale Av BER PR5 .....33 F1
Stephenson St CHLYE PR6 .....45 E3
Stevenson Av LEYL PR25 .....36 A1
Stewart St PRES PR1 .....2 A5
Stiles Av KIRK/FR/WA PR4 .....22 A5
Stirling Cl CHLYE * PR6 .....45 E3
   LEYL PR25 .....36 A3
Stockdale Crs BER PR5 .....33 D2
Stocks Rd FUL/RIB PR2 .....17 G2
Stocks St PRES PR1 .....2 D2
Stokes Hall Av LEYL PR25 .....35 G4
Stonebridge Cl BER PR5 .....32 A1
Stonebridge Ter
   GAR/LONG * PR3 .....15 B3
Stone Cft PRES PR1 .....2 D2
Stonecroft Rd LEYL PR25 .....34 D5
Stonefield KIRK/FR/WA PR4 .....28 B2
   PRES PR1 .....24 A2
Stonefold Av KIRK/FR/WA PR4 .....22 A5
Stonehouse Gn CHLYE PR6 .....37 F1
Stone Park Rd GAR/LONG PR3 .....6 C2
Stoney Butts FUL/RIB PR2 .....16 B3
Stoneygate PRES PR1 .....3 G4
Stoney Holt LEYL PR25 .....36 C3

Stoney La BER PR5 .....32 A3
Stonyhurst CHLY/EC PR7 .....47 G1
Stour Ldg FUL/RIB PR2 .....11 G2
Strand Rd PRES PR1 .....2 B5
Strand St West FUL/RIB * PR2 .....17 G3
Stratfield Pl LEYL PR25 .....35 H3
Stratford Dr FUL/RIB PR2 .....11 H4
Stratford Rd CHLYE PR6 .....44 D4
Strathmore Gv FUL/RIB PR2 .....44 B3
Strathmore Rd FUL/RIB PR2 .....12 A4
Stricklands La PRES PR1 .....23 H2
Strutt St PRES PR1 .....18 D2
Stryands FUL/RIB PR4 .....22 A5
Stuart Cl FUL/RIB PR2 .....13 G5
Stuart Rd FUL/RIB PR2 .....13 G5
Studfold CHLY/EC PR7 .....40 B5
Studholme Av PRES PR1 .....24 A4
Studholme Cl FUL/RIB PR2 .....24 A4
Studholme Crs PRES PR1 .....24 A3
Stump La CHLYE PR6 .....44 D2
Sturminster Cl PRES PR1 .....24 A4
Suffolk Rd PRES PR1 .....18 C2
Sulby Dr FUL/RIB PR2 .....13 H3
Sulby Gv FUL/RIB PR2 .....14 A3
Summerfield LEYL PR25 .....35 F1
Summerfield Cl PRES PR1 .....24 C4
Summer Trees Av FUL/RIB PR2 .....10 B5
Sumner St LEYL PR25 .....35 G3
Sumpter Cft PRES PR1 .....24 A4
Sunbury Av PRES PR1 .....23 H3
Sunningdale GAR/LONG PR3 .....6 B2
Sunny Brow CHLY/EC PR7 .....47 E3
Surgeon's Ct PRES PR1 .....2 E4
Surrey St PRES PR1 .....19 E3
Sussex St PRES PR1 .....18 C2
Sutcliffe St CHLY/EC PR7 .....44 D3
Sutton Dr FUL/RIB PR2 .....16 B3
Sutton Gv CHLYE PR6 .....41 F3
Swallow Av PRES PR1 .....24 A2
Swallow Ct CHLYE PR6 .....37 G3
Swallowfields KIRK/FR/WA PR4 .....10 C3
Swallowfold FUL/RIB PR2 .....9 H4
Swansea St FUL/RIB PR2 .....17 G2
Swansey La CHLYE PR6 .....37 E3
Swan St PRES PR1 .....3 K2
Swarbrick Ct GAR/LONG PR3 .....15 C3
Swill Brook La PRES PR1 .....19 E5
Swords Cross Cl CHLY/EC PR7 .....44 A5
Sycamore Av CHLY/EC PR7 .....39 F4
Sycamore Ct FUL/RIB PR2 .....13 E2
Sycamore Ct CHLY/EC PR7 .....44 B5
Sycamore Dr PRES PR1 .....24 A2
Sycamore Rd CHLYE PR6 .....40 D5
   FUL/RIB PR2 .....13 E2
Syke Hl PRES PR1 .....3 H5
Syke St PRES PR1 .....3 H5
Sylvancroft FUL/RIB PR2 .....11 E3
Sylvan Gv BER PR5 .....26 A4
Symonds Rd FUL/RIB PR2 .....12 A5

T

Tabley La KIRK/FR/WA PR4 .....5 G5
Tag Cft FUL/RIB PR2 .....10 D3
Tag Farm Ct FUL/RIB PR2 .....10 D3
Tag La FUL/RIB PR2 .....10 D2
Talbot Dr CHLY/EC PR7 .....39 G2
Talbot Rd LEYL PR25 .....2 B4
   PRES PR1 .....2 B4
   PRES PR1 .....24 A1
Talbot Rw CHLY/EC * PR7 .....43 F3
Talbot St CHLYE * PR6 .....45 E1
   FUL/RIB PR2 .....11 H5
Tamar Cl LEYL PR25 .....35 H5
Tamar St PRES PR1 .....19 G3
Tanglewood Rd FUL/RIB PR2 .....12 D3
Tanhouse La CHLYE PR6 .....41 F1
Tansley Av CHLY/EC PR7 .....46 B4
Tanterton Hall Rd FUL/RIB PR2 .....10 D4
Tanyard Cl CHLY/EC PR7 .....46 B5
Tan Yard La GAR/LONG PR3 .....15 D2
Tarn Cl PRES PR1 .....22 D2
Tarn Hows Cl CHLY/EC * PR7 .....44 B5
Tarradale KIRK/FR/WA PR4 .....28 B2
Taunton St PRES PR1 .....19 F2
Taylor St CHLY/EC PR7 .....44 B3
   PRES PR1 .....2 B6
Tay St PRES PR1 .....2 B7
Teal Cl LEYL PR25 .....19 E1
Tees St PRES PR1 .....19 E1
Teil Gn FUL/RIB PR2 .....13 G2
Temperance St CHLYE PR6 .....45 E2
Temple Ct PRES PR1 .....41 G4
Temple Flds CHLYE * PR6 .....41 G4
Temple Wy CHLYE PR6 .....40 D4
Tenby Rd PRES PR1 .....3 H6

Tennyson Av CHLY/EC PR7 .....44 C4
Tennyson Mill Ct PRES PR1 .....19 F2
Tennyson Pl BER PR5 .....25 F4
Tennyson Rd PRES PR1 .....19 F2
Tenterfield St PRES PR1 .....3 F3
Terrace St PRES PR1 .....19 E2
Teven St BER PR5 .....25 G5
Theatre St PRES PR1 .....2 E5
Thirlmere Cl KIRK/FR/WA PR4 .....28 B2
Thirlmere Dr GAR/LONG PR3 .....15 A5
Thirlmere Rd CHLY/EC PR7 .....44 A4
   PRES PR1 .....19 H2
Thistle Cl CHLYE PR6 .....45 E2
Thistlecroft FUL/RIB PR2 .....11 E3
Thistleton Rd FUL/RIB PR2 .....16 C2
Thomas St PRES PR1 .....3 K5
Thompson St PRES PR1 .....19 F1
Thornfield Av FUL/RIB PR2 .....13 H5
   GAR/LONG PR3 .....15 B2
Thorngate PRES PR1 .....23 F2
Thorngate Ct PRES PR1 .....23 F2
Thornhill Rd CHLYE PR6 .....40 D5
   LEYL PR25 .....34 C4
Thornley Pl CHLYE PR6 .....14 A5
Thornley Rd FUL/RIB PR2 .....14 A5
Thornpark Dr FUL/RIB PR2 .....16 B3
Thorn St PRES PR1 .....19 E1
Thornton Av FUL/RIB PR2 .....11 F4
Thornton Dr BER PR5 .....27 E3
   CROS/BRETH PR26 .....31 E5
Thorntrees Av FUL/RIB PR2 .....16 B2
Thorpe Cl PRES PR1 .....18 B2
Threefields FUL/RIB PR2 .....11 E3
Three Nooks BER PR5 .....33 G4
Threlfall CHLY/EC PR7 .....39 H5
Threlfall St CHLY/EC PR7 .....17 C2
Thropps La KIRK/FR/WA PR4 .....29 A3
Thurnham Rd FUL/RIB PR2 .....16 C3
Thurston Rd LEYL PR25 .....35 G3
Tiber St PRES PR1 .....3 J5
Tinkerfield Cl PRES PR1 .....12 A1
Tinniswood Cl CHLY/EC PR7 .....44 B5
Tintern Av CHLY/EC PR7 .....44 D5
Titan Wy CROS/BRETH PR26 .....34 B3
Tithe Barn La CHLY/EC PR7 .....38 B3
   CHLYE PR6 .....41 G3
Tithebarn St PRES PR1 .....3 G3
Tiverton Cl FUL/RIB PR2 .....7 F5
Todd La North BER PR5 .....25 G3
Todd La South BER PR5 .....32 A1
Tollgate PRES PR1 .....24 A2
Tolsey Dr KIRK/FR/WA PR4 .....22 B4
Tom Benson Wy FUL/RIB PR2 .....10 D1
Tomlinson Rd FUL/RIB PR2 .....17 G1
   LEYL PR25 .....35 F2
Tootell St CHLY/EC PR7 .....44 B4
Tootle Rd GAR/LONG PR3 .....15 C2
Top Acre KIRK/FR/WA PR4 .....22 A5
Topaz Wy CHLYE PR6 .....45 E4
Tormore Cl CHLYE PR6 .....41 G4
Tower Gn FUL/RIB PR2 .....12 B1
Tower La FUL/RIB PR2 .....12 B1
Tower Vw PRES PR1 .....17 G4
Town Brow CHLYE PR6 .....36 D2
Towneley Rd GAR/LONG PR3 .....15 B3
Towneley Rd West
   GAR/LONG * PR3 .....15 B3
Townfield Cl KIRK/FR/WA PR4 .....28 B3
Towngate CHLY/EC PR7 .....42 B2
   LEYL PR25 .....35 F5
Town La CHLYE PR6 .....37 G5
Townlea Cl PRES PR1 .....23 E3
Townley La PRES PR1 .....22 B2
Townley St CHLYE PR6 .....44 D3
Townsway BER PR5 .....32 A1
Trafalgar Cl FUL/RIB PR2 .....11 H5
Trafalgar St CHLY/EC PR7 .....44 C1
Trafford St PRES * PR1 .....18 A1
Tramway La BER PR5 .....33 F3
Tranmoor KIRK/FR/WA PR4 .....28 B4
Travers Pl FUL/RIB PR2 .....17 G2
Trawden Crs FUL/RIB PR2 .....13 G4
Trent St GAR/LONG PR3 .....15 A3
The Triangle FUL/RIB PR2 .....12 A4
Trinity Fold PRES * PR1 .....3 F2
Trinity Pl PRES * PR1 .....3 F3
Trinity Rd CHLY/EC * PR7 .....44 B3
Tristan Av KIRK/FR/WA PR4 .....28 C5
Troon Cl CHLYE PR6 .....39 F3
Troon Ct PRES PR1 .....17 G5
Troutbeck Pl FUL/RIB PR2 .....13 G3
Troutbeck Rd CHLY/EC PR7 .....44 B5
Trout St PRES * PR1 .....19 E4
Trower St PRES PR1 .....3 K6
Truro Pl PRES PR1 .....19 F2
Tudor Av FUL/RIB PR2 .....16 A1
   PRES PR1 .....19 H3
Tudor Cft BER PR5 .....32 A2

Tuer St LEYL PR25 ....35 F2
Tulketh Av FUL/RIB PR2 ....17 F2
Tulketh Brow FUL/RIB PR2 ....17 G2
Tulketh Crs FUL/RIB PR2 ....17 G2
Tulketh Rd FUL/RIB PR2 ....17 F2
Tunbridge Pl PRES PR1 ....19 F2
Tunley Holme BER PR5 ....33 F4
The Turbary FUL/RIB PR2 ....11 G5
Turks Head Yd PRES PR1 ....3 G4
Turnbury Cl CHLYE PR6 ....39 F3
Turner Av BER PR5 ....31 G3
Turner St PRES PR1 ....3 H1
Turnfield FUL/RIB PR2 ....10 D2
The Turnpike FUL/RIB PR2 ....11 H2
Turpin Green La LEYL PR25 ....35 H3
Turton Dr CHLYE PR6 ....45 E1
Tuson Cft KIRK/FR/WA PR4 ....28 B2
Tuson Dr PRES PR1 ....2 C2
Two Acre La PRES * PR1 ....23 G5
Tyne St BER PR5 ....25 H5
   PRES PR1 ....2 B7

U

Ullswater Rd CHLYE/EC PR7 ......44 B4
   FUL/RIB PR2 ....13 E4
Under Wd FUL/RIB PR2 ....11 G5
Union St CHLYE/EC PR7 ....44 C1
   CHLYE PR6 ....37 G4
   PRES PR1 ....2 E3
Uplands Cha FUL/RIB PR2 ....11 F2

V

The Vale FUL/RIB PR2 ....12 B3
Valentines La KIRK/FR/WA PR4 ...10 C4
Valentines Meadow
   KIRK/FR/WA PR4 ....10 C4
Valley Rd GAR/LONG PR3 ....15 D3
   PRES PR1 ....23 H1
Valley Vw CHLYE PR6 ....45 E3
   FUL/RIB PR2 ....12 C4
Valley View Rd BER PR5 ....24 C3
Varley St PRES PR1 ....18 C1
Ventnor Pl FUL/RIB PR2 ....11 E4
Ventnor Rd CHLYE/EC PR7 ....44 A5
Vernon St PRES PR1 ....18 B2
Vevey St LEYL PR25 ....35 G4
Vicarage Cl CHLYE/EC PR7 ....39 F3
   FUL/RIB PR2 ....12 B4
Vicarage La BER PR5 ....21 E3
   FUL/RIB PR2 ....12 B4
Vicarage St CHLYE PR6 ....44 D1
Vicarsfields Rd LEYL PR25 ....35 G5
Victoria Ct GAR/LONG PR3 ....6 C3
Victoria Pde FUL/RIB PR2 ....17 F2
Victoria Park Av FUL/RIB PR2 ....16 B2
   LEYL PR25 ....34 C5
Victoria Park Dr FUL/RIB PR2 ....16 B2
Victoria Quay FUL/RIB PR2 ....17 E4
Victoria Rd BER PR5 ....25 F1
   FUL/RIB PR2 ....12 B5
Victoria St BER PR5 ....31 H1
   CHLYE/EC PR7 ....44 D1
   GAR/LONG PR3 ....15 B3
   PRES PR1 ....3 H1
Victoria Ter CHLYE PR6 ....44 D1
Village Cft CHLYE/EC PR7 ....39 E4
Village Dr FUL/RIB PR2 ....19 H1
Village Green La FUL/RIB PR2 ....10 D2
The Villas KIRK/FR/WA PR4 ......10 C3
Villiers Ct PRES PR1 ....18 A1
Villiers St PRES * PR1 ....17 H1
   PRES PR1 ....18 A1
The Vinery KIRK/FR/WA PR4 .....29 D1
Vine St CHLYE/EC PR7 ....44 C1
   PRES PR1 ....2 B3

W

Waddington Rd FUL/RIB PR2 .....20 A1
Wadham Rd PRES PR1 ....3 J6
Waingate FUL/RIB PR2 ....9 G4
Waldon St PRES PR1 ....19 F2
Walgarth Dr CHLYE/EC PR7 ......44 A3
Walkdale KIRK/FR/WA PR4 ....22 B4
Walker La FUL/RIB PR2 ....11 E1
Walker Pl PRES PR1 ....3 J4
Walker St PRES PR1 ....3 H2
The Walled Gdn CHLYE PR6 ......40 B1
Wallend Rd FUL/RIB PR2 ....16 B4
Walletts Rd CHLYE/EC PR7 ......44 B4

Walmer Gn KIRK/FR/WA PR4 .....28 B5
Walnut Cl PRES PR1 ....23 F3
Walton Av PRES PR1 ....23 F3
Walton Gn BER PR5 ....25 F2
Walton's Pde PRES PR1 ....2 D5
Walton Summit Rd BER PR5 ......33 E3
Walton Vw PRES PR1 ....19 F3
Wanstead St PRES PR1 ....19 G3
Warbury St PRES PR1 ....19 G2
Wardle Ct CHLYE PR6 ....40 C1
Ward's End PRES PR1 ....3 G4
Ward St BER PR5 ....31 H2
   CHLYE PR6 ....45 E3
Warner Rd PRES PR1 ....19 F3
The Warren FUL/RIB PR2 ....13 F2
Warton Pl CHLYE/EC PR7 ....44 A2
Warton St PRES * PR1 ....2 C7
Warwick Cl FUL/RIB PR2 ....12 A4
Warwick Rd BER PR5 ....25 F2
   CHLYE/EC PR7 ....42 C3
   LEYL PR25 ....35 E5
Warwick St FUL/RIB PR2 ....15 B2
   PRES PR1 ....2 E2
Wasdale Cl LEYL PR25 ....38 D1
Wasdale Gv GAR/LONG PR3 ......15 A5
Washington La CHLYE/EC PR7 ....39 H5
Waterford Cl FUL/RIB PR2 ....13 E3
Watering Pool La BER PR5 ....24 D5
Water La FUL/RIB PR2 ....17 G3
Waterloo Rd FUL/RIB PR2 ....17 F1
Waterloo St CHLYE/EC PR7 ......44 C1
Waterloo Ter FUL/RIB PR2 ....17 G2
Water's Edge FUL/RIB PR2 ....10 D5
Water St BER PR5 ....25 G4
   CHLYE/EC PR7 ....44 C2
Watery La FUL/RIB PR2 ....17 F3
   PRES PR1 ....19 F3
Watkin La BER PR5 ....31 H2
Watkin Rd CHLYE PR6 ....37 H3
Watling Street Rd FUL/RIB PR2 ..12 A5
   FUL/RIB PR2 ....13 E4
Waverley Dr KIRK/FR/WA PR4 ...29 D2
Waverley Gdns FUL/RIB PR2 .....19 G1
Waverley Rd PRES PR1 ....19 F2
The Weald KIRK/FR/WA PR4 .....10 B3
Weaver's Brow CHLYE PR6 ....45 F4
Webster St PRES PR1 ....17 G2
Weeton Rd FUL/RIB PR2 ....16 C2
Weirden Cl PRES PR1 ....23 G5
Weld Av FUL/RIB PR2 ....44 C5
Weldbank La CHLY/EC PR7 ....44 C5
Weldbank St FUL/RIB PR2 ....44 C5
Wellbrow Dr GAR/LONG PR3 .....15 C2
Wellfield KIRK/FR/WA PR4 ....28 B1
Wellfield Av LEYL PR25 ....35 F5
Wellfield Rd BER PR5 ....31 G2
   PRES PR1 ....2 B3
Wellington Av LEYL PR25 ....35 H4
Wellington Pl BER PR5 ....25 F4
Wellington Rd FUL/RIB PR2 ......17 F2
Wellington St CHLYE/EC PR7 ....44 C1
   PRES PR1 ....2 A2
Well Orch BER PR5 ....33 F4
Wells Fold Cl CHLYE PR6 ....37 G3
Wells St PRES PR1 ....19 F3
Welsby Rd LEYL PR25 ....34 D4
Wembley Av PRES PR1 ....23 F1
Wensley Pl FUL/RIB PR2 ....13 F4
Wentworth Cl PRES PR1 ....17 E5
Wentworth Dr CHLYE PR6 ....39 F3
   GAR/LONG PR3 ....6 C2
Werneth Cl PRES PR1 ....24 B5
Wesley St BER PR5 ....32 D1
West Av FUL/RIB PR2 ....11 E2
West Bank CHLYE/EC PR7 ....44 B4
Westbourne Rd CHLYE/EC PR7 ..44 B4
Westbrook Crs FUL/RIB PR2 .....11 E4
Westby Pl FUL/RIB PR2 ....16 D2
West Cliff PRES PR1 ....2 C6
West Cliff Ter PRES PR1 ....2 D6
West Crs GAR/LONG PR3 ....6 C2
West Dr LEYL PR25 ....36 B1
West End PRES PR1 ....17 E5
Westend Av CHLYE/EC PR7 ......46 B4
Westerlong FUL/RIB PR2 ....16 B2
Western Dr LEYL PR25 ....34 D3
Westfield BER PR5 ....31 G1
Westfield Dr BER PR5 ....26 D5
   FUL/RIB PR2 ....13 G4
   LEYL PR25 ....34 D3
Westgate FUL/RIB PR2 ....11 H3
   LEYL PR25 ....35 E5
Westlands CROS/BRETH PR26 ...34 F1
Westleigh Ms KIRK/FR/WA * PR4 ..10 A4
Westleigh Rd FUL/RIB PR2 ....16 D2
West Meadow FUL/RIB PR2 ......10 C5
Westminster Pl CHLYE/EC PR7 ...42 A2
   KIRK/FR/WA PR4 ....22 B5

Westminster Rd CHLYE/EC PR7 ..44 C3
Westmorland Cl PRES PR1 ....23 F2
Weston St FUL/RIB PR2 ....2 B2
West Paddock LEYL PR25 ....35 E4
West Park Av FUL/RIB PR2 ....16 D1
West Park La FUL/RIB PR2 ....17 E1
West Rd FUL/RIB PR2 ....12 B5
West Sq KIRK/FR/WA PR4 ....28 C2
West Strd PRES PR1 ....2 A2
West St CHLYE/EC PR7 ....44 C3
West Vw BER PR5 ....32 C2
   KIRK/FR/WA PR4 ....28 C2
   PRES PR1 ....19 E1
West View Ter FUL/RIB PR2 ......17 G3
West Wy CHLY/EC PR7 ....40 A5
Westway FUL/RIB PR2 ....12 C4
Westwell Rd CHLYE PR6 ....44 D1
Westwood Rd BER PR5 ....33 G5
   LEYL PR25 ....35 G2
Wetherall St FUL/RIB PR2 ....17 H2
Whalley Rd BER PR5 ....21 H1
Whalley St BER PR5 ....25 H4
   CHLY/EC * PR7 ....44 C3
Wham Hey KIRK/FR/WA PR4 .....30 A2
Wham La KIRK/FR/WA PR4 ......29 A5
   KIRK/FR/WA PR4 ....30 A2
Wharfedale Av FUL/RIB PR2 ......13 G3
Wharfedale Cl LEYL PR25 ....38 C1
Wheatfield CROS/BRETH PR26 ...34 A4
Wheatley Dr GAR/LONG PR3 .....15 B3
Wheatsheaf Av GAR/LONG PR3 ..15 B3
Wheelton La LEYL PR25 ....35 G2
Whernside Crs FUL/RIB PR2 ......13 F3
Whernside Wy LEYL PR25 ....36 A3
Whimberry Cl CHLYE PR6 ....45 E2
Whinfield Av CHLYE PR6 ....44 D1
Whinfield La FUL/RIB PR2 ....16 D3
Whinfield Pl FUL/RIB PR2 ....16 D3
Whinneyfield La
   KIRK/FR/WA PR4 ....5 F3
Whinny La CHLYE/EC PR7 ....39 G4
Whinsands Cl FUL/RIB PR2 ....13 F3
Whitby Av FUL/RIB PR2 ....10 D3
Whitby Pl FUL/RIB PR2 ....10 D4
Whitebeam Cl PRES PR1 ....23 G5
Whitefield Meadow BER PR5 .....25 H4
Whitefield Rd PRES PR1 ....23 E2
Whitefield Rd East PRES PR1 .....23 E2
Whitefield Rd West PRES PR1 ....23 E2
Whitefriar Cl FUL/RIB PR2 ....11 E3
White Gate Fold CHLY/EC PR7 ...46 C3
Whiteholme Rd FUL/RIB PR2 .....16 C2
White Meadow FUL/RIB PR2 .....10 C5
Whitendale Dr BER PR5 ....32 D2
Whitethorn Cl CHLYE PR6 ....37 E2
Whitethorn Sq FUL/RIB PR2 .....16 B2
Whitmore Dr FUL/RIB PR2 ....20 A1
Whitmore Gv FUL/RIB PR2 ....20 A1
Whitmore Pl FUL/RIB PR2 ....19 H1
Whittam Rd FUL/RIB PR2 ....44 B5
Whittingham La FUL/RIB PR2 .....9 F3
Whittingham Rd GAR/LONG PR3 ..15 A3
Whittle Gn KIRK/FR/WA PR4 ......5 G2
Whittle Hl KIRK/FR/WA PR4 ......5 G2
Whittle Pk CHLYE PR6 ....37 F2
Whitworth Dr CHLY/EC PR7 ......44 A4
Wholesome La KIRK/FR/WA PR4 ..29 C3
Wigan Rd CHLY/EC PR7 ....39 E4
   CHLYE PR6 ....39 E1
Wignall St PRES * PR1 ....19 E2
Wigton Av LEYL PR25 ....34 D5
Wilbraham St PRES PR1 ....19 E2
Wilderswood Cl CHLYE PR6 ......37 G2
Wildman St PRES PR1 ....18 A1
Wilkinson St BER PR5 ....31 H1
Willacy La KIRK/FR/WA PR4 ......4 A2
William Henry St PRES PR1 ....19 E3
Williams La FUL/RIB PR2 ....13 E1
William St BER * PR5 ....31 G1
William Young Cl PRES * PR1 ....19 E1
Willow Cl BER PR5 ....27 E5
   BER PR5 ....31 G1
   PRES PR1 ....23 E2
Willow Coppice FUL/RIB PR2 .....10 C5
Willow Crs FUL/RIB PR2 ....19 F1
   LEYL PR25 ....36 B1
Willow Dr CHLY/EC PR7 ....46 B2
Willow Fld CHLYE PR6 ....37 G1
Willow Field Cha BER * PR5 ......27 H4
Willow Gn FUL/RIB PR2 ....17 E3
Willow Rd CHLYE PR6 ....41 E5
The Willows CHLYE/EC PR7 ......47 F1
Willows Park La GAR/LONG PR3 ..15 C2
Willow Tree Av GAR/LONG PR5 ...6 D2
Willow Tree Crs LEYL PR25 ......34 D3
Willow Wy KIRK/FR/WA PR4 .....29 D2
Wilmar Rd LEYL PR25 ....36 A2
Wilmot Rd FUL/RIB PR2 ....13 G5

Wilton Gv PRES PR1 ....
Wilton Pl LEYL * PR25 ....
Wiltshire Ms KIRK/FR/WA PR4 ....
Winckley Rd PRES PR1 ....
Winckley Sq PRES PR1 ....
Windermere Av LEYL PR25 ....
Windermere Rd CHLYE * PR6 ....
   FUL/RIB PR2 ....
   PRES PR1 ....
Windflower Dr LEYL PR25 ....
Windsor Av FUL/RIB PR2 ....
   GAR/LONG PR3 ....
   KIRK/FR/WA PR4 ....
   PRES PR1 ....
Windsor Cl CHLYE/EC PR7 ....
   LEYL PR25 ....
Windsor Dr FUL/RIB PR2 ....
Windsor Rd BER PR5 ....
   CHLY/EC PR7 ....
   CHLYE/EC PR7 ....
Winery La BER PR5 ....
Wingates PRES PR1 ....
Winmarleigh Rd FUL/RIB PR2 ....
Winslow Cl PRES PR1 ....
Winsor Av LEYL PR25 ....
Winster Cl BER PR5 ....
Winter Hill Cl FUL/RIB PR2 ....
Winton Av FUL/RIB PR2 ....
Withnell Gv CHLYE PR6 ....
Withy Grove Cl BER PR5 ....
Withy Grove Crs BER PR5 ....
Withy Grove Rd BER PR5 ....
Withy Pde FUL/RIB PR2 ....
Withy Trees Av BER PR5 ....
Withy Trees Cl BER PR5 ....
Witton St PRES PR1 ....
Woburn Gn LEYL PR25 ....
The Wold CHLYE PR6 ....
Wolseley Cl LEYL PR25 ....
Wolseley Pl PRES * PR1 ....
Wolseley Rd PRES PR1 ....
Wolseley Ter PRES PR1 ....
Woodacre Rd FUL/RIB PR2 ....
Wood Bank PRES PR1 ....
Woodcock Fold CHLYE/EC PR7 ....
Woodcroft Cl PRES PR1 ....
Wood End PRES PR1 ....
Wood End Rd CHLYE PR6 ....
Woodfall CHLY/EC PR7 ....
Woodfield BER PR5 ....
Woodfield Rd CHLYE/EC PR7 ....
Woodford Copse CHLY/EC PR7 ....
Wood Gn LEYL PR25 ....
Woodhall Crs BER PR5 ....
Woodhart La CHLY/EC PR7 ....
Woodland Gv PRES PR1 ....
The Woodlands FUL/RIB PR2 ....
Woodlands Av BER PR5 ....
   FUL/RIB PR2 ....
   PRES PR1 ....
Woodlands Dr FUL/RIB PR2 ....
   LEYL PR25 ....
Woodlands Meadow
   CHLY/EC PR7 ....
Woodlands Wy KIRK/FR/WA PR4 ....
Woodlea Rd LEYL PR25 ....
Woodmancote CHLY/EC PR7 ....
Woodplumpton La
   GAR/LONG PR3 ....
Woodplumpton Rd
   FUL/RIB PR2 ....
   FUL/RIB PR2 ....
   KIRK/FR/WA PR4 ....
Woods Gn PRES PR1 ....
Woodside CHLY/EC PR7 ....
   LEYL PR25 ....
Woodside Av CHLYE PR6 ....
   FUL/RIB PR2 ....
   FUL/RIB PR2 ....
   KIRK/FR/WA PR4 ....
Woodstock Cl BER PR5 ....
Woodvale CROS/BRETH PR26 ....
Woodvale Rd BER * PR5 ....
Woodville Rd CHLY/EC * PR7 ....
   PRES PR1 ....
Woodville Rd West PRES PR1 ....
Woodville St LEYL PR25 ....
Woodway FUL/RIB PR2 ....
Wookey Cl FUL/RIB PR2 ....
Worcester Av LEYL PR25 ....
Worden Cl LEYL PR25 ....
Worden La LEYL PR25 ....
Worden Rd FUL/RIB PR2 ....
Wordsworth Pl BER PR5 ....
Wordsworth Ter CHLYE PR6 ....
Worthing Rd FUL/RIB PR2 ....
Worthy St CHLYE PR6 ....
Wren Av PRES PR1 ....

Index - featured places

Lancashire Records Office
PRES PR1............................ 2 C4
Lancaster Lane Primary School
LEYL PR25.......................... 36 B3
Lane Ends Trading Estate
FUL/RIB PR2 .... 17 G1
Lea Endowed CE
Primary School
KIRK/FR/WA PR4............... 10 A4
Lea Primary School
FUL/RIB PR2 .... 16 B2
Lever House Primary School
LEYL PR25.......................... 36 A1
Leyland Golf Club
LEYL PR25.......................... 36 B4
Leyland Leisure Centre
LEYL PR25.......................... 35 F4
Leyland Methodist J & I School
LEYL PR25.......................... 35 H3
Leyland St Marys Catholic
Technology College
LEYL PR25.......................... 35 E5
Light Industrial Estate
KIRK/FR/WA PR4............... 28 B5
Lisieux Hall Hospital
CHLYE PR6.......................... 37 E4
Little Hoole Primary School
KIRK/FR/WA PR4............... 28 C5
Little Theatre
CHLY/EC PR7...................... 44 C2
Longridge CE Primary School
GAR/LONG PR3 .... 15 B3
Longridge Gm Primary School
GAR/LONG PR3 .... 15 B2
Longridge Health Centre
GAR/LONG PR3 .... 15 C3
Longridge High School &
Sports Centre
GAR/LONG PR3 .... 15 B4
Longsands Community Primary
School *FUL/RIB* PR22......... 13 F3
Longton County Primary School
KIRK/FR/WA PR4............... 28 C2
Longton Health Centre
KIRK/FR/WA PR4............... 28 C1
Lostock Hall Community
High School
BER PR5.............................. 25 E5
Lostock Hall Primary School
BER PR5.............................. 24 D5
Manchester Mill
Industrial Estate
PRES PR1............................ 19 E3
Manor Road Primary School
CHLYE PR6.......................... 37 F2
Market Halls
PRES PR1............................ 3 F3
Market Walk Shopping Centre
CHLY/EC PR7...................... 44 C2
Mayfield School
CHLY/EC PR7...................... 44 C5
Middleforth CE Primary School
PRES PR1............................ 23 H3
Moorbrook School
FUL/RIB PR2 .... 12 A5
Moorfield School
PRES PR1............................ 12 C5
Moor Hey School
BER PR5.............................. 24 C5
Moor Nook Primary School
FUL/RIB PR2 .... 14 A5
Moor Park High School
PRES PR1............................ 18 C1
Moss Side Industrial Estate
CROS/BRETH PR26............. 34 C1
Moss Side Primary School
CROS/BRETH PR26............. 34 B3
Muslim Girls Secondary School
PRES PR1............................ 3 K1
National Football Museum
PRES PR1............................ 18 D1
The Natural Health Centre
PRES PR1............................ 3 H2
New Cemetery
FUL/RIB PR2 .... 19 G2
New Longton CE
Primary School
KIRK/FR/WA PR4............... 29 D2
New Mill Industrial Estate
BER PR5.............................. 32 D2
Northbrook Primary School
LEYL PR25.......................... 35 F3
Novotel
BER PR5.............................. 32 D3
Old Brewery Trading Estate
PRES PR1............................ 2 B3
Old Mill Industrial Estate
BER PR5.............................. 25 F5

Old Mill Leisure Club
CHLYE PR6.......................... 45 F4
Open Market
PRES PR1............................ 3 F3
Otters Leisure Pool
GAR/LONG PR3 .... 7 E3
Our Lady & St Edwards RC
Primary School
GAR/LONG PR3 .... 6 D5
Our Lady & St Gerards RC
Primary School
BER PR5.............................. 31 G1
Our Ladys RC High School
FUL/RIB PR2 .... 11 G3
Oxhey Trading Estate
PRES PR1............................ 17 H1
Palace Cinema
GAR/LONG PR3 .... 15 C3
Parker Street Industrial Estate
FUL/RIB PR2 .... 17 H2
Parklands High School
CHLY/EC PR7...................... 44 A2
Penwortham Cricket Club
PRES PR1............................ 24 A2
Penwortham Girls High School
PRES PR1............................ 23 G1
Penwortham Golf Club
PRES PR1............................ 17 F4
Penwortham Holme Recreation
Centre
PRES PR1............................ 2 A7
Penwortham Primary School
PRES PR1............................ 23 E1
Penwortham Sports Club
PRES PR1............................ 24 A2
Pines Hotel
CHLYE PR6.......................... 33 F5
Playhouse Theatre
PRES PR1............................ 2 E3
Pool House Primary School
FUL/RIB PR2 .... 11 E2
Post Graduate Medical Centre
FUL/RIB PR2 .... 12 B4
Premier Lodge
BER PR5.............................. 32 B2
CHLYE PR6.......................... 41 E2
CHLYE PR6.......................... 45 E5
Preston Bowl
PRES PR1............................ 17 H1
Preston College
FUL/RIB PR2 .... 12 C3
Preston Crematorium
FUL/RIB PR2 .... 14 C3
Preston Cricket Club
PRES PR1............................ 24 A1
Preston Golf Club
FUL/RIB PR2 .... 12 D3
Preston Grasshoppers RFC
KIRK/FR/WA PR4............... 6 B5
Preston Marriott Hotel
GAR/LONG PR3 .... 6 D3
Preston North End FC (Deepdale)
PRES PR1............................ 18 D1
Preston Sports Arena
KIRK/FR/WA PR4............... 10 C5
Preston Sports Club
PRES PR1............................ 2 D7
Primrose Hill Primary School
CHLY/EC PR7...................... 38 D3
Priory High School
PRES PR1............................ 23 E1
The Priory Pool
PRES PR1............................ 22 D1
Queens Drive Primary School
FUL/RIB PR2 .... 11 H3
Queens Retail Park
PRES PR1............................ 3 J3
Red Rose Radio Station
PRES PR1............................ 3 H2
Red Scar Industrial Estate
FUL/RIB PR2 .... 14 B3
Ribbleton Avenue County Infant
School
PRES PR1............................ 19 E1
Ribbleton Avenue
Methodist Junior School
PRES PR1............................ 19 F1
Ribbleton Hall High School
FUL/RIB PR2 .... 13 H5
Ribbleton Hospital
FUL/RIB PR2 .... 19 H1
Ribbleton Lane Trading Estate
PRES PR1............................ 3 J2
Ribble Village Health Centre
FUL/RIB PR2 .... 19 G1
Riverside Medical Centre
BER PR5.............................. 25 F1

The Roebuck Primary School
FUL/RIB PR2 .... 17 H1
Roman Way Industrial Estate
FUL/RIB PR2 .... 14 C1
Royal Cross Primary School
FUL/RIB PR2 .... 16 C2
Royal Preston Hospital
FUL/RIB PR2 .... 12 B2
The Ryan Medical Centre
BER PR5.............................. 25 G5
Sacred Heart Catholic
Primary School
FUL/RIB PR2 .... 17 G2
Sacred Heart RC Primary School
CHLYE PR6.......................... 45 E3
St Aidans Primary School
BER PR5.............................. 25 H5
St Andrews CE Infant School
LEYL PR25.......................... 35 F4
St Andrews CE Primary School
FUL/RIB PR2 .... 17 F2
St Annes Catholic Primary School
LEYL PR25.......................... 34 D4
St Anthonys RC Primary School
FUL/RIB PR2 .... 11 G4
St Augustines RC Primary School
PRES PR1............................ 3 H5
St Bedes RC Primary School
BER PR5.............................. 33 F5
St Bernards Catholic
Primary School
FUL/RIB PR2 .... 16 A2
St Catherines RC Primary School
LEYL PR25.......................... 36 A2
St Cecilias RC High School
GAR/LONG PR3 .... 15 B4
St Chads RC Primary School
CHLYE PR6.......................... 41 F1
St Clares Catholic
Primary School
FUL/RIB PR2 .... 12 B2
St Georges CE Primary School
CHLY/EC PR7...................... 45 E5
St Georges Shopping Centre
PRES PR1............................ 3 F4
St Gregorys Catholic
Primary School
CHLY/EC PR7...................... 44 C5
St Gregorys RC Primary School
PRES PR1............................ 12 D5
St Ignatius RC Primary School
PRES PR1............................ 3 G1
St James CE Primary School
CHLYE PR6.......................... 45 E3
CROS/BRETH PR26............. 34 A4
St Johns Shopping Centre
PRES PR1............................ 3 G3
St Josephs Catholic
Primary School
CHLYE PR6.......................... 40 D5
St Josephs C Primary School
PRES PR1............................ 19 E2
St Leonards CE Primary School
BER PR5.............................. 25 E2
St Maria Goretti RC
Primary School
FUL/RIB PR2 .... 13 H3
St Mary Magdalen RC
Primary School
PRES PR1............................ 24 A2
St Marys CE Primary School
CHLY/EC PR7...................... 42 C4
St Marys Health Centre
PRES PR1............................ 23 F1
St Marys Primary School
LEYL PR25.......................... 35 F3
St Marys RC Primary School
CHLY/EC PR7...................... 44 A3
St Marys & St Benedicts RC
Primary School
BER PR5.............................. 25 G5
St Matthews CE Primary School
PRES PR1............................ 19 F3
St Michaels CE High School
CHLYE PR6.......................... 40 C5
St Oswalds RC Primary School
CHLY/EC PR7...................... 46 A5
KIRK/FR/WA PR4............... 29 A1
St Patricks RC Primary School
BER PR5.............................. 25 G1
St Pauls CE Primary School
CROS/BRETH PR26............. 31 F2
St Peters CE Primary School
CHLYE PR6.......................... 41 E5
FUL/RIB PR2 .... 12 B1
St Pius X Preparatory School
FUL/RIB PR2 .... 12 A3

St Stephens CE Primary School
PRES PR1............................
St Teresas RC Primary School
PRES PR1............................
PRES PR1............................
St Wilfreds RC Primary School
GAR/LONG PR3 ....
Samlesbury CE Primary School
BER PR5..............................
Sandy Lane Clinic
LEYL PR25..........................
Sharoe Green Hospital
FUL/RIB PR2 ....
Shaw Hill Hotel Golf &
Country Club
CHLYE PR6..........................
Shay Lane Industrial Estate
GAR/LONG PR3 ....
Sherburn School
PRES PR1............................
Sherwood Primary School
FUL/RIB PR2 ....
Southlands High School
CHLY/EC PR7......................
South Ribble Industrial Estate
BER PR5..............................
South Ribble Museum &
Exhibition Centre
LEYL PR25..........................
Springfield Industrial Estate
PRES PR1............................
Starkie Industrial Estate
FUL/RIB PR2 ....
Stonehouse School
PRES PR1............................
Swallow Hotel
BER PR5..............................
Talbot Road Industrial Centre
CROS/BRETH PR26.............
Tardygate Trading Estate
BER PR5..............................
Tennis Centre
BER PR5..............................
Towngate Healthcare Clinic
LEYL PR25..........................
Traceys Industrial Estate
LEYL PR25..........................
Travel Inn
FUL/RIB PR2 ....
Travelodge
CHLYE PR6..........................
Tulketh Community
Sports College
FUL/RIB PR2 ....
UCI Cinema
FUL/RIB PR2 ....
University of Central Lancashire
PRES PR1............................
PRES PR1............................
Vehicle Museum
LEYL PR25..........................
Virgin Active Swimming Pool
BER PR5..............................
Walton Le Dale High School
BER PR5..............................
Walton Le Dale Primary School
BER PR5..............................
Walton Le Dale School Clinic
BER PR5..............................
Warner Village Cinema
BER PR5..............................
Wellfield Business Park
PRES PR1............................
Wellfield High School
LEYL PR25..........................
West View Leisure Centre
PRES PR1............................
Westwood Primary School
BER PR5..............................
Whitefield Primary School
PRES PR1............................
Whittingham Hospital
GAR/LONG PR3 ....
Whittle Le Woods CE
Primary School
CHLYE PR6..........................
Woodlea Junior School
LEYL PR25..........................
Woodplumpton St Annes CE
Primary School
KIRK/FR/WA PR4...............
Worden High School
LEYL PR25..........................
Zakariya School
PRES PR1............................

Acknowledgements

The Post Office is a registered trademark of Post Office Ltd. in the UK and other countries.

Schools address data provided by Education Direct.

Petrol station information supplied by Johnsons

One-way street data provided by © Tele Atlas N.V. Tele Atlas

Garden centre information provided by:

Garden Centre Association Britains best garden centres

Wyevale Garden Centres

Notes

 **Street by Street** QUESTIONNAIRE

Dear Atlas User
Your comments, opinions and recommendations are very important to us.
So please help us to improve our street atlases by taking a few minutes
to complete this simple questionnaire.

You do NOT need a stamp (unless posted outside the UK). If you do not want to remove this page from your street atlas, then photocopy it or write your answers on a plain sheet of paper.

Send to: The Editor, AA Street by Street, FREEPOST SCE 4598,
Basingstoke RG21 4GY

ABOUT THE ATLAS...

Which city/town/county did you buy?

Are there any features of the atlas or mapping that you find particularly useful?

Is there anything we could have done better?

Why did you choose an AA Street by Street atlas?

Did it meet your expectations?

Exceeded ☐   **Met all** ☐   **Met most** ☐   **Fell below** ☐

Please give your reasons

 ML226

continued overleaf

Where did you buy it?

For what purpose? (please tick all applicable)

To use in your own local area ☐   **To use on business or at work** ☐

Visiting a strange place ☐   **In the car** ☐   **On foot** ☐

Other (please state)

LOCAL KNOWLEDGE...

Local knowledge is invaluable. Whilst every attempt has been made to make the information contained in this atlas as accurate as possible, should you notice any inaccuracies, please detail them below (if necessary, use a blank piece of paper) or e-mail us at *streetbystreet@theAA.com*

ABOUT YOU...

Name (Mr/Mrs/Ms)
Address
                                                    Postcode
Daytime tel no
E-mail address

Which age group are you in?

Under 25 ☐   **25-34** ☐   **35-44** ☐   **45-54** ☐   **55-64** ☐   **65+** ☐

Are you an AA member?   **YES** ☐   **NO** ☐

Do you have Internet access?   **YES** ☐   **NO** ☐

Thank you for taking the time to complete this questionnaire. Please send it to us as soon as possible, and remember, you do not need a stamp (unless posted outside the UK).

ML